T0113462

DO YOU KNOW WHAT TO DO WHEN . . .

- Your toddler hits his baby sister?
- The preschool teacher tells you your daughter is biting other children?
- Your 4-year-old is taking longer and longer each night to get ready for bed?
- You call your son for dinner, but he ignores you and continues playing?
- During a walk in the park, your 2-year-old pulls loose from your hand and starts running away?
- Your 5-year-old calls you stupid?

These are the behaviors that test your patience—and your parenting skills. By using the 30 parenting tools provided by expert Virginia K. Stowe, you'll feel confident when faced with the stressful situations that need effective actions and results. You'll also discover the all-day-long approach that helps a child grow with self-esteem, structure, and a firm idea of what's right and wrong. And best of all, instead of nagging, you and your child will have time for all the laughter and fun of these precious early years.

TIRED OF NAGGING?
The better way to become a great parent

BANTAM BOOKS
New York   Toronto   London   Sydney   Auckland

TIRED
OF
NAGGING?

30 Days to Positive Parenting

Virginia K. Stowe, M.S.N.

WITH

Andrea Thompson

TIRED OF NAGGING?

A Bantam Book / June 1998

All rights reserved.

Copyright © 1998 by Virginia Stowe.

Library of Congress Cataloging-in-Publication Data
Stowe, Virginia K.
Tired of nagging?: 30 days to positive parenting / Virginia K. Stowe
with Andrea Thompson.
p.   cm.
Includes bibliographical references (p. 205) and index.
ISBN 978-0-553-37915-0
1. Parenting—United States.   2. Achievement motivation in children—United States.
3. Child psychology—United States.   I. Thompson, Andrea.   II. Title.
HQ755.8.S765   1998
649'.1—dc21   97-51246
                                                                              CIP

Published simultaneously in the United States and Canada

Bantam Books are published by Bantam Books, a division of Bantam Doubleday Dell
Publishing Group, Inc. Its trademark, consisting of the words "Bantam Books" and the
portrayal of a rooster, is Registered in U.S. Patent and Trademark Office and in other
countries. Marca Registrada. Bantam Books, 1540 Broadway, New York, New York 10036.

146688838   BVG   01

Dedication

To the mothers and fathers I've worked with . . . who raise their children with commitment, reflection, humor and a truly inspiring willingness to keep growing and learning themselves.

To Douglas Brinton Stowe and Emily Augusta Thompson . . . two great people who have given us more joy and added more depth to our lives than they would ever imagine.

Acknowledgments

First and foremost, my thanks to the many mothers and fathers who have taken part in my workshops and groups over the years. I'm grateful for the opportunity to have worked with them and for all they've helped me to understand about the challenges, struggles, and satisfactions of today's parenting. Those parents' stories and experiences, with names and other identifying characteristics changed for privacy's sake, are the heart and soul of this book.

I've been fortunate enough to know and learn from some wise and generous people, notably: Dr. Carol Hartman, my supervisor at the Intensive Nursing After-Care Project funded by the National Institute of Health under the auspices of Harvard Medical School at Massachusetts Mental Health Center, who led me through my earliest professional contacts with parents and children; Dr. Nina Lief, clinical director of the Early Childhood Development Center, New York Medical College, whose insights into how children grow and change during the first three years of life shaped my own ideas about effective parenting skills; Dr. Edwin Church, my friend and colleague, who helped this book come into being by always telling me I had something good and useful to say.

I am grateful to the University of Pennsylvania Graduate School of Nursing and Psychiatry where I studied, especially for its emphasis on normal child development and preventive mental health care, which is at the core of what I both practice and promote.

My great appreciation to Amy Berkower and Karen Solem of Writers House, who liked the book from the start and offered valuable suggestions on how best to present it, and to my editor, Beth de Guzman, whose enthusiasm has been most encouraging and indispensable.

Thanks to several fine friends: Barbara Wolf, Ronnie Jankoff and Mary Cohen, who supplied fabulous real-life examples of parent-child hassles and helped me settle on a title, and Lovejoy Duryea, who has been encouraging me for years to sit down and start writing.

A final thank you to my husband, Rick, not least of all for having tolerated a dining room table half covered with my papers and notes during the many months TIRED OF NAGGING? was coming to life.

Contents

Chapter 1

TIRED OF NAGGING?:

An Introduction.

A 1½-YEAR-OLD, who normally loves going out for a leisurely walk, suddenly wants nothing to do with getting in her stroller. Mom wrestles her child in, amidst screams, kicks, and arching back.

A 2-year-old refuses to take Dad's hand as they're walking to the park. Dad clamps on even tighter. As soon as he loosens his grip, off goes his toddler, gleefully running away while the frantic father charges after.

A 3-year-old has demanded SpaghettiOs and fish sticks for dinner—then won't eat.

A 5-year-old thinks her parents are "so stupid," and tells them so.

Does any of that sound familiar? Have you been there? Preschool-aged children are wonderful and trying little human beings! As we watch them grow from squirming newborns to young children heading off for the first day of kindergarten, they enchant and delight us. And just as often, they drive us nuts. Why is it so hard to get them to do the simple things they need to do? Why do we get caught up in so many struggles all day long? What more do they want from us anyway?

I know what you want, because it is what every parent wants: You want your child to behave in the ways that lead him steadily forward, toward his own life. You want him to learn to talk, dress himself, share his toys, play nicely with other children, use the toilet, not run into the street, accept what he has to do, challenge what seems wrong to him . . . and, in time, do his homework, be responsible to himself and others, leave home, get a job, get married. *You want him to become independent.*

Here's what your child wants: All those same things! He wants to get on with his own life. *He wants to be independent.*

Since you and your youngster have the same goal, being a parent should be easy. As you know, however, it's often not easy at all.

WHAT HE DOES THAT YOU CAN'T STAND; WHAT YOU DO THAT YOU CAN'T STAND

Growing up to the age of 5 is heady business. Your youngster in those years is learning (besides the walking, talking, eating, toileting basics) that some things are safe and some are dangerous, that Mom and Dad are perfect and then that Mom and Dad aren't so perfect, that other kids exist in the world and sometimes they're fun and sometimes they're hateful, that he doesn't know how to do a lot of things he wants to do, and on and on.

All this, at times, makes him angry, frustrated, scared, exhausted, impetuous, or in some other way bothered by his current lot in life. Those feelings often lead to whining, dawdling, hitting, the "NO's," plain orneriness, and other (to you) unpleasant activities. But your child has to act in those ways. They are natural behaviors and they are not bad. They are what he uses to try to get what he wants or needs.

They are also, of course, the kinds of behaviors that drive you up the wall and that make a lot of the time you spend with your child not as agreeable as you wish it would be. They are the kinds of behaviors that so easily lead you to act in ways that you don't like and would prefer not to—nagging your child, being the policeman and issuing orders, sometimes losing it and shouting.

DEMOCRACY AT WORK

It is absolutely in your power to eliminate much of the whining, dawdling, demandingness, nagging, and yelling that interfere with the joy and pleasure you have in being a parent—and that make your child's march toward independence more unruly, and perhaps less successful, than it need be.

How to get more agreeably from here to there is what this book will show you. It represents, really, a democratic kind of child-raising.

When you are overly permissive—when you give in to the demands or the dawdles—you give your power away to your child. He's calling the shots. When you are overly authoritarian, you're calling the shots—you keep all the power. In our democratic system, you share power with your child: Sometimes you insist that he behave in certain ways, even if he is not in a mood or finds it difficult to comply. Other times you honor his wishes or requests.

PARENTING TOOLS OF THE TRADE:
THE 30 ESSENTIALS

Learning how to share the power is really what this book is about.

First, understand where your child is at different stages in his young life, and that's going to change and shift a lot over the course of these 5 years. Bring your expectations in line with his capabilities and needs, and you've made a major move toward reducing the struggles. The next section of this book gives you a quick-and-easy overview of these "ages and stages" from babyhood to age 5.

Second, use parenting tools that work; that's the focus of the central part of this book. You could just as easily call these skills or tips, but I like the idea of tools. It suggests something sturdy, useful, practical, enduring.

There are 30 tools—all of them describing ways you can change your approach in order to promote in your youngster the behaviors you want from him. Some of them suggest small (or maybe they'll be radical) shifts in the way you *view* your child, in *how you see* why he's probably acting the way he's acting. Some of them suggest changes in *how you say things* to your child or in *how you spend time together*.

I'll give you examples of the tools in action. I'll use the most common kinds of behaviors (at each age) from your child that give you grief. And I'll provide little miniscripts that suggest solutions. In most cases, you'll want to use two or four or five tools. Of course, your own real-life interactions with your youngster won't follow these scenarios word for word, but if you adapt the approaches to suit your child's situation, you'll be pleased at how often you get the results you're after.

MAKE THIS BOOK YOUR
TRAVELING COMPANION

Take *Tired of Nagging?* with you when you're closing yourself in the bathroom for 15 minutes. Read a couple of pages while you're waiting for the bus. Spend 15 minutes a day looking over some of the ideas presented here. Think of it, if you like, as a 30-day parenting shape-up course, and each day for one month take a few minutes reading about, thinking about, or trying out one of the 30 tools.

You probably have a shelf full of child-raising guidebooks, big books that explore and explain all aspects of your child's development. They have their place. Use the fat books for your backup, your encyclopedias, your reference library. Use this book as your traveling companion.

I have kept it, I hope, easy to read and understand, because I've learned from the many mothers and fathers I've worked with in my twenty-five years as a parent-child educator that they too often feel overwhelmed by theory and analysis from the "experts." I want this to be a simple little book that says, in effect: Perhaps this is what's going on that's making you struggle too much with your child, and perhaps this is what you can do differently to stop some of the struggles.

When parents start to use these tools, they can't get over how much more fun they have with their youngsters. They just are not struggling with their kids so much, even when those children are in their most difficult, most stubborn stages. The whole tone of family life shifts to a level where everyone is happier, where there's a calmer, more cooperative spirit in the air.

Try it—and you'll see.

Chapter 2

BEHAVIORAL AGES AND STAGES:

A <u>very</u> short course in what's going on with your child, from infancy to age 5.

IF YOU <u>EXPECT</u> YOUR CHILD to bring his dinner plate over to the sink and rinse it, and he doesn't do so, you feel annoyed and inclined to nag him about the matter.

If you *don't expect* such behavior of your child, because you know he's not tall enough yet to reach the sink and he hasn't yet learned to turn faucets on and off, you don't feel annoyed and naggy that he doesn't get the plate where it belongs.

Keeping your expectations for your child's behavior in line with his capabilities and needs is the biggest solution to reducing frustrations (on both sides, yours and his) and the nagging that so often follows. Sometimes that's easy: You understand, for example, that he's too short to do this or that. Other times, knowing what can and can't be expected of your child as he develops is a trickier business; his abilities or needs keep changing, and they're not always so obvious.

In this chapter, you'll find a brief overview of typical behaviors, needs, and accomplishments of the child up to age 5.

Consider it a road map to where your child is at in several areas of development, a road map that you may find useful in figuring out why he does what he does. (Of course, each child grows in his own way, at his own pace; every child won't fall neatly into every time frame listed here.)

6 MONTHS TO 1 YEAR

Language[1]

🖝 Cries when hungry, tired, wet, or bored (cry is baby's first language).

🖝 Babbles (ah-ah, mah-mah, dah-dah).

🖝 Makes single-syllable sounds (dah, bah, kah, mah).

🖝 Looks at you when you talk.

🖝 Understands about 8 to 14 words by the end of the first year (Mommy, Daddy, bye-bye, baby, shoe, ball, cookie, juice, names of family pets).

🖝 May say Mama, Dada, ba (bottle), ca (car).

Learning

🖝 Has an attention span of about 5 minutes; demands change of activities about every 10 minutes.

🖝 Has no object permanence (knowing that something or someone exists even when out of sight) until about age 1.

Psychological/Social

🖝 Experiences anxiety at around 6 to 8 months when separated from main caregiver.

🖝 Experiences stranger anxiety at around 6 to 8 months.

🖝 Develops a sense of security or trust (major achievement).[2]

Physical

🖝 Starts reaching and grabbing between 5 and 6 months.

🖝 Can pull herself up to a sitting position by 6 months.

🖝 Rolls over completely in any direction.

🖝 Generally crawls on all fours.

🖝 Pulls up to a standing position by 12 months.

🖝 Sits well by the end of the first year.

🖎 Toward the end of the first year, can turn toys over and activate some items by pushing buttons.
🖎 May cruise (hold on to surfaces to help her walk from place to place).
🖎 May walk independently by the end of the first year.
🖎 Imitates some actions, like waving.
🖎 Can use pincer grasp (thumb and index finger) to pick up small objects.

Self-Help

🖎 Can hold her own bottle, possibly a sippy cup.
🖎 May hold a spoon by the end of the first year, but needs help to use it.
🖎 Has no urinary or bowel control.

1 YEAR TO 18 MONTHS

Language

🖎 By 18 months, may be able to say 10 to 20 words, understands considerably more.
🖎 Experiences great frustration (resulting at times in temper tantrums) at not being able to make herself understood.

Learning

🖎 Needs to explore for intellectual development (includes exploring cabinets, wastebaskets, and drawers).[3]
🖎 Doesn't understand the consequences of her behavior (getting into dangerous situations, breaking things).
🖎 Has a short attention span, sometimes 10 or 15 minutes.
🖎 Does not yet understand or respond predictably to "No."
🖎 Sense of time is limited to the present; little awareness of past or future; can sometimes respond to "now."

Psychological/Social

🖎 Temper tantrums start at around 12 to 14 months, and occur off and on until the child is 4 or older.

🖎 Separation anxiety may reappear between 17 and 22 months.

🖎 Slaps back if slapped.

🖎 No awareness of sharing. Demands personal attention.

Physical

🖎 Stands, cruises, toddles, climbs: Grabs and touches everything.

🖎 Can open and close container lids; put blocks, spoons, or other items inside a jar and then remove them.

🖎 Likes to pour, turn hinged items, push, pull.

🖎 Can sit on and push a kiddie car with feet.

🖎 Can manage some finger foods by herself.

Self-Help

🖎 Can hold cup.

🖎 Uses spoon without help, but smears food when feeding self.

🖎 May cooperate when being dressed.

🖎 No urinary or bowel control.

18 MONTHS TO 2 YEARS

Language

🖎 May be able to talk, or will demonstrate understanding by following directions and responding to requests.

🖎 Can name almost everything she sees on a daily basis.

🖎 Actively imitates words. Forms 2-word sentences.

🖎 Has an expressive vocabulary of 50 or more words.

🖎 Uses pronouns indiscriminately.

🖎 Listens to and enjoys simple stories.

🖎 May be able to give her first and last names.

Learning

📖 Can match familiar objects.
📖 Can distinguish between "one" and "many."
📖 Still has a limited sense of time; can understand "now" and "soon" (helpful in learning to wait).
📖 Can identify some body parts.
📖 Does extensive observing or staring.

Psychological/Social

📖 Likes to control others and order them around.
📖 Can't share possessions yet.
📖 Can communicate some feelings and desires by words or gestures.
📖 Can occasionally put someone else's wishes above her own.
📖 Prefers a relationship with one adult at a time.
📖 No manners yet (interrupts, doesn't say hello).[4]
📖 Refuses to eat or has strong preferences.
📖 May have separation anxiety again.
📖 Sibling rivalry very intense.

Physical

📖 Walks evenly.
📖 Runs, but generally has difficulty starting and stopping with ease; jumps clumsily.
📖 By 2 years, may be trusted alone on stairs.
📖 Has fully developed right- or left-handedness.
📖 Can make a crude V stroke in drawing.
📖 Turns pages of a book one at a time.

Self-Help

📖 Can zip and unzip large zipper.
📖 Can pick up and put away some toys if asked to.
📖 Participates in washing.
📖 Can help undress self.
📖 May verbalize toilet needs.

2 TO 3 YEARS

Language

🖉 Vocabulary is growing, even if she doesn't use it.

🖉 Asks questions.

🖉 By 3 years, uses 3- to 4-word sentences.

🖉 Is receptive to someone else's spoken observations and ideas.

Learning

🖉 Attention span is still limited, 10 to 15 minutes.

🖉 Still has a limited sense of time; understands "today," "soon," "in a minute," and closer to age 3, may understand "tomorrow."

🖉 During the second half of this year, her desire to do everything for herself greatly intensifies, although abilities haven't caught up with desire. The result: temper tantrums.

Psychological/Social

🖉 Still can't share; goes through "I, my, mine" stage with everything she sees and wants.[5]

🖉 Likes to be with other children, but requires adult supervision to avoid pushing, hitting, and so on.

🖉 At $2^1/2$, very demanding about who does what when.

🖉 At $2^1/2$, frequently refuses to eat.

🖉 Fears are common during the latter part of the year, including fear of the dark, animals, water, nighttime.

🖉 Sometimes remembers to say "hello" and "good-bye" and "please" and "thank you."[6]

🖉 Has difficulties with siblings.

Physical

✍ Climbs, investigates, examines, takes things apart (but has trouble putting things back together), pokes into all openings.

✍ Explores, wanders, runs ahead, hides (may run off from caregiver and hide under clothes rack in the store).

✍ Jumps; hops on one foot and then the other.

✍ Throws and retrieves all sorts of objects.

✍ Can turn pages one at a time, grasp a crayon or spoon, turn a doorknob.

✍ Needs lots of space for play and the opportunity to create her own territory.

Self-Help

✍ Uses a spoon and fork for eating, but often still stuffs her mouth with food.

✍ Gaining ability to hold urine for 1 to 2 hours and have regular bowel movements; close to age 3, may be receptive to toileting suggestions.

3 TO 3¹/₂ YEARS

Language

✍ Knows about 900 words.

✍ Asks lots of "what" and "why" questions.

✍ Interested in animal stories, here-and-now stories.

Learning

✍ Has an attention span of at least 15 to 20 minutes.

✍ Increased concentration makes memory games, like Picture Lotto, possible.

✍ Has a growing sense of time—yesterday, today, tomorrow.

✍ Enjoys mock adult activities, like playing store and hospital, preparing dinner; plays with blocks and other building materials to create towns, garages, race tracks.

✍ Can match shapes.

Psychological/Social

✍ More easygoing; improved relationship with parents.

✍ Has some understanding of right from wrong.

✍ Peers become more important; increased skills aid in better friendships.

✍ Is beginning to share and understand the concept of taking turns.

✍ May have imaginary friends (for companionship and/or blaming for wrongdoings).

✍ May have fears, and try to overcome them by telling scary stories with aggression or disaster themes.[7]

Physical

✍ Has greatly increased mastery over body; can run, walk forward, backward, and sideways, kick a ball, catch a ball if arms are outstretched.

✍ Can gallop, jump, or run to music.

✍ Fine motor coordination has improved; can piece together puzzles and pick up small objects with ease.

✍ Can manage scissors to some extent.

✍ Pedals a tricycle and steers to avoid obstacles.

Self-Help

✍ Uses a spoon and fork.

✍ Can undress and often dress herself; still needs help with shoelaces and buttons.

✍ Can control bowels and bladder during the daytime and get to the toilet.

3¹/₂ TO 4 YEARS

Language and Learning

✐ Knows about 1,500 words by age 4.
✐ Improved pronunciation helps her be better understood.
✐ Begins to understand that words represent feelings as well as things.
✐ May use nasty words to let off steam when angry.
✐ Can sort objects by appearance, use, and feel.

Psychological/Social

✐ Often says "No" again, perhaps related to anxiety, fears, and indecision.
✐ Struggles against routines, such as dressing, bathing, eating, going to bed.
✐ Has an increased understanding of right from wrong.
✐ Heightened language skills enable her to recruit or exclude other children in play.
✐ Asks questions about bowels, genitals, and sexuality issues; starts to look at parents when they are undressed; wants to observe other children for physical differences (doctor play with other children often begins).
✐ May have fears—of the dark, animals, grotesque faces.

Physical

✐ Runs smoothly.
✐ May sometimes stumble, may lose fine muscle coordination for drawing and building, because of trying to accomplish things too quickly.
✐ Likes to catch and throw balls.
✐ Hops.
✐ Can cut with scissors.
✐ Growth changes may cause some eye-blinking or poor visual coordination.

Self-Help

✍ Fussy eating starts again.

✍ Is usually dry during the day and often at night; situations of stress may cause her to revert to soiling again, which usually won't last more than a month.

✍ Can dress herself except for shoelaces and buttons.

✍ Is beginning to develop an ability for self-discipline.

4 TO 5 YEARS

Language

✍ Knows 1,500 to 2,200 words by age 5.

✍ Is verbally adept, plays with words; still learning by imitating others.

✍ Knows and may use four-letter (swear) words, toilet talk.

Learning

✍ Asks many and more complex questions, out of curiosity and to garner attention.

✍ Tells imaginative stories, often with make-believe details or violent descriptions.

✍ Is hazy sometimes about the difference between fantasy and reality.

✍ Improved coordination, spatial understanding, and attention span allow for elaborate building with Lego, Tinkertoys, Lincoln Logs, Brio trains, and the like.

✍ Responds appropriately to parent's limitations ("Go only as far as Julie's yard," for example).

Psychological/Social

✍ Highly sociable, and prefers peers over adults.

✍ Two may gang up on a third.

✍ May be able to settle many of her own disagreements or difficulties with friends.

✍ May deliberately initiate disruptive behavior.

✍ Has a sense of humor, reflected in silliness.

✍ May boast, brag, and make lots of noise.

✍ Likes dramatic play, real or imagined, which depicts her view of experiences, ideas, feelings, situations.

✍ Likes superhero roles and talk; takes on superhero or other characters as a way of practicing different roles in society.

✍ Has greater awareness of what parents consider right and wrong and what is approved or disapproved of.

✍ May lie or steal (believes possession is ownership).

✍ Has questions about marriage, where babies come from.

Physical

✍ Can climb trees and ladders, go up the down slide.

✍ Displays physical habits like nail-biting, nose-picking, hair-twirling.

✍ Is very interested in the bodily differences between boys and girls.

✍ May play doctor with other children.

✍ May masturbate.

✍ Can cut a line with scissors.

✍ Can draw a human figure, including eyes, hair, ears, hands, and feet.

✍ Can copy the letters O, V, H, T.

Self-Help

✍ Can dress herself.

✍ Can use fork and spoon but not knife.

✍ Can wash hands, brush teeth (with some supervision).

✍ Toilet trained, though may still need help with wiping, and still some nighttime wetting (up to age 5 or 6).

Chapter 3

THE 30 PARENTING TOOLS

SOME OF THE TOOLS I talk about—such as assuming that your child really does want to cooperate and remembering that change takes time (and tomorrow your child will still be with you)—are, so to speak, just for you. They're about attitude and consciousness. Give them some thought as you read them, and later on, a few minutes' reflection on those days when parenting is wearing you down. You'll feel more kindly disposed toward your temporarily terrible two, or impossibly bossy 5-year-old!

Some of the tools are about the time you spend with your child—get outdoors a lot, do 20 minutes of one-on-one play-time each day.

Most of the 30 tools are the ones you will apply when you reach one of those standoffs with your child that can so easily lead to frustration, anger, and nagging.

What makes the tools effective has to do with a major shift in the way you perceive and interact with your child. Once you change from the authoritative mode to the democratic mode, once you're no longer saying, "I'm overpowering you" and instead are saying, "What's going wrong here? What's holding us up? What are *we* going to do to make this better?" then your child is involved in solving the problem also. Then you're both on the same wavelength.

THE 30 TOOLS

> **Assume your child wants to cooperate; assume you both really are on the same side.**

This is the cardinal tool, the one that makes all the others possible and sensible. At the same time, many parents, I have discovered, find it difficult to believe.

Does the following scene strike a familiar chord?: It's six P.M. and you've got dinner on the table. Macaroni and cheese, your child's favorite meal. You call him to come and eat, and you call again and then again. He's deeply engrossed in snapping Legos together in alternating lines of red, yellow, and blue, and acts as if he doesn't hear you. You lose patience and shout: "Dinner! Now! I mean it!" Each of you is annoyed with the other, because each of you—it seems—wants something different.

In fact, *in the bigger picture*—and despite all those ornery, difficult, pushing-up-against-you behaviors—you and your youngster really both want the same thing, which is your child's independence. At this particular moment, for example, he wants to be independent enough to keep stacking Legos and you want him to be independent enough to understand that he needs to stop that for now and have something to eat.

Now picture this scene: You've put the food on the table and your spouse is deeply engrossed in trying to finish a report for work. Your attitude and your approach in summoning your spouse to dinner would be very different, wouldn't they? If your spouse doesn't jump at first call, you wouldn't assume your generally cooperative, grown-up spouse is being difficult and defiant. You would say, "Please finish up in the next few minutes," not announce, "Dinner! Now!"

As long as parents are convinced their youngster is simply trying to defy them, they will use all kinds of ways to be authoritative and in control. Once they realize that *they and their child have a common goal,* the parents are able to change their approaches. They're able to think, What can I do here that's going to make it possible for my child to go along with what I want?

And then the parents might find most helpful some of the tools we'll talk about. They can provide transitions: "You can have five more minutes playing, and then I'll call you again for dinner." They can show their child empathy and give him hope: "I know how hard it is to leave those Legos right now. You can come right back to them as soon as we finish dinner."

Children *really do want to cooperate.* First, your youngster wants to please you; it's just that his desire to explore and to function on his own often outweighs his desire for your approval. Second, he has learned, at least by the time he's about 3 years old, that by doing what Mom or Dad wants, he gets more freedom! He sees that it's in his own best interest to go along with his parents' requests in a timely fashion, because the more he does so, the more independence and rights he gains. (But he does also want to save a little face while he's doing all that complying!)

I have seen this demonstrated so often among the parents in my workshops: Realize that you and your child have a common goal, that you're both on the same track, and everything becomes so much easier.

> **Each day, spend 20 minutes of uninterrupted time with your child. Follow her lead and do something she wants to do.**

Early mornings are good. Wake yourself and your youngster up 20 minutes before all the hurly-burly of getting everybody out of the house has to start, and spend that time together. Maybe she'd like you to read to her. Maybe she wants you both to climb back into bed and listen to the birds outside.

Afternoons or early evenings—when you and your child reconnect after she gets home from preschool or you're just back from work—are good too. She needs you then; she's waited a long time already and doesn't want to wait any longer.

Here's how to work it: First, give yourself a small transition time before you reach the household: Get off the bus or car-pool vehicle three blocks sooner, amble a bit, look in some shop windows. If you drive your own car, stop at a neighborhood park for a few minutes, or pull over a couple of blocks from your home. And then when you are home, *don't* do what you feel like doing or think you ought to be doing, which probably is to pour yourself a glass of wine or make a cup of tea, check the mail, get the chicken into the oven. Just be with your child.

Plop down on the floor and let her show you how to stack blocks, if that's what she feels like doing. Maybe she wants to sit in your lap and talk. Or take a walk around the block. Blot out all the other things on your mind, forget your to-do list, and spend these minutes on her turf and at her rhythm.

This sounds easy. *It's not.* In my workshops, parents who have tried it tell me that 20 minutes feels like forever! They can't believe how tough it is for them! That's because it's rare that we give our youngsters undivided attention.

Think of the last time you and your child were together for

the whole day. Chances are that time was spent taking her along with you to the supermarket, delivering her to a play date, talking to her while you put in a load of laundry, and in other ways *being together while one or two other things were going on or getting accomplished.* This is fine and necessary, but it's not the same as giving your child undivided attention.

The more those parents in my workshops try the 20 minutes, the better they get at tuning out the distractions and focusing on their child. And they reap splendid benefits.

The point is, your youngster knows you care about her when you are willing to give her your complete attention doing something she feels like doing. Imagine a close friend of yours has time only for a quick phone chat with you, but does have time for lunch with another friend. You would feel less cared for. As an adult, you might tell your friend how you feel. If you were a *child,* you might misbehave to get the attention you need.

When you give your child your undivided attention, she knows you care. And when she is filled up with you, when she has had you all to herself for a while, then she will give you *your* time. She won't have to whine and pull at your leg while you're trying to start dinner or make a phone call, because you've already given her a piece of yourself. And when sibling rivalry is hot and heavy in your home, giving yourself exclusively to each child for 20 minutes will work wonders.

Try it today. And the next day. It may take you a while to get in the rhythm of being with your child in this way, of slowing down your own "getting on with business" motor and being open to her. But you'll get better at it.

Provide plenty of outside time.

I'm sure that from the earliest weeks of your child's life, you learned the pleasures and benefits of getting outdoors together as often as possible.

It's nice for you: Pack up your little one and head out for a walk to the park or to meet a friend for half an hour at your local coffee bar, and you enjoy a quick fix for those housebound, stir-crazy feelings that can so easily beset new parents.

It's nice for your baby: The one activity guaranteed to calm a fussy, crying infant, so many parents say, is to tuck him into the stroller or settle him in the car seat and go out for a walk or drive. The pleasant feel of air wafting over his body, or the lulling effect of the car's movement, almost always soothes and relaxes.

As your child grows through the toddler and preschool years, outside time becomes even more important. During these years (and, of course, for many more to come), your youngster has an enormous amount of energy to expend. But he also needs to practice a number of physical skills—running, jumping, climbing, and skipping.

The key word is, he *needs* to do those things. They are as vital to his growth as learning to manage a fork and spoon, brush his teeth, and get his feet into his socks and shoes. He feels, in his body and soul, the need to run, jump, climb, and skip, and he will relish many opportunities to do so. In fact, if he doesn't get those opportunities, if he doesn't have lots of chances to run, jump, climb, and skip, *he'll be more likely to act up and misbehave at home.*

I urge parents to fit outside time with a child into their schedules as religiously as they plan for reading a book together or telling bedtime stories. If you live in a house with a fenced-in and safe backyard, let your youngster loose to run as often as possible. If you live in a city apartment, go to the park, a playground, or one of the marvelous new indoor play spaces, where your child can practice his physical skills.

Before the age of 3, he will need some help and supervision, especially with climbing. One father of a 2½-year-old took his son every morning to the local reservoir, where there were both a running track and a series of steps. For 10 to 15 minutes, the little boy went happily up and down the steps, holding his dad's hand; when he'd had his fill of climbing stairs, his father strapped him into his special three-wheeled jogger's stroller and together they took off for a couple of laps around the reservoir.

There's another plus to outside time. You know that if you're mad at your spouse and you go for a walk and a little cooling off, you come home feeling better. The same benefits hold true for parent and child. If you and your youngster have been having an especially trying day, go out somewhere together. Any change of scene tends to restore positive, pleasant feelings. And if you can get in some running, climbing, jumping, and skipping, all the better.

As often as possible, give your child the power to make her own choices and to be in control.

Offering choices is one of the most powerful tools at your disposal, and it's really so simple. Let your 2-year-old decide if she'll have milk or juice when she's thirsty or if she wants to take Kermit the Frog or Big Bird to bed. Let your 3-year-old choose the shirt she'll wear to school. Let your 4-year-old pick a play date for the afternoon. Let your 5-year-old help plan one or two dinners for next week. If you do this, you'll find many of the minor power struggles of the day go away, or at least decrease in strength and length.

In Chapter 4, you'll see that offering choices is often part of navigating the typical parent-child battles that lead to nagging. So many of those battles—all of them, when you think about it—have at the core a need or desire for control. The parent needs to be in control of the child—to keep her from getting hurt, to make sure she eats properly, dresses warmly, and gets enough sleep. The child wants to be in control of herself—because she's on her personal road to independence.

But during her first five years of life, there are so many ways in which your child feels out of control.

At ages 1½ to 2½ the world is bursting open for her. She's beginning to understand the possibilities, but doesn't yet have the capabilities. Just pulling a shirt over her own head and getting the arms in the armholes is tough! She understands how doors open but doesn't have the strength and manual agility to turn a knob. She knows what she wants but doesn't have the words to ask for it. She's often frustrated throughout the day, because there's so much she can't do. (She's a "terrible two"!)

She begins preschool, and suddenly she's spending several hours a day with a bunch of other little kids who want many of the same things she does. She has to follow a schedule that's out of her control.

Perhaps a younger sibling enters the picture and is soon crawling around and becoming a real presence, and she's jolted from her familiar position in the family.

And from time to time, just as she's feeling on top of the game and in charge, something pops up to take away her feelings of control. Here's an example: A 4½-year-old boy went with his parents, avid amateur sailors, on a weekend sail. Because of unexpectedly rough water, the boy had to remain harnessed to the side of the boat throughout the trip. For three or four days after the cruise, he was in a ferociously defiant mood. When Mom announced dinner, for example, he ran out into the backyard. The mother wisely realized her young son needed to reassert his autonomy and feel in control again, so she gave him some time to comply.

Throughout these early years, keep giving your child choices as often as possible. Recognize what he can do at any given point and let him do it. Avoid power struggles in which the outcome really doesn't make a difference one way or another.

Let your child know you've noticed his good, kind behavior.

If you're like most parents, it's your child's difficult or unruly actions that get your attention. You'll say: "Stop fighting with your brother," but might not think of saying, "Gee, that was nice, the way you and your brother played together all afternoon."

It *is* important to compliment a child when he's been able to correct a negative behavior. If he and his brother have been battling tooth and nail for days, if you've spoken to him about this unhappy state of affairs and helped him to figure out ways to improve it, if he has clearly tried and is making progress, of course he deserves your good words. Later in this section, we talk about the importance of praising a child when praise is due.

But what I'm getting at here is something a little different. Give your child a pat on the back from time to time just on general principle—not because he's changed something you didn't like, but because he's getting things right to begin with. And children do. As they keep learning and growing, they get many things right, in ways that make them a pleasure to behold and fun to be with.

A father in one of my groups became sensitive to the difference between praising after improved behavior and praising on general principle. He says: "So often Max gets our praise because he's being nicer to his sister or he's remembered to do one of the little chores we give him. I always have a feeling that we're manipulating him—like giving a dog a treat biscuit when he's learning to sit or heel!"

Max's father looked for other "general principle" times to compliment his son. After a nice, chatty dinner one evening, for example, he said to Max: "I really enjoyed this supper with you. I liked hearing about your train layout and telling you about my day." That kind of remark is a natural response to a small, pleasant moment that's going on and that your child is part of.

As you look for those ways to let your child know you've noticed his nice behavior, also think of how you might encourage such behavior. Maybe you have your toddler join you in his high chair at the dinner table each evening. And maybe, each evening, after a few calm minutes, he pushes his spoon over the edge of his chair, plops his hand in his food, and makes silly sounds, or in other ways goes off on his own, to your disappointment.

Your very young child probably doesn't know how to get into the act. See how you might include him and make him an active participant in the dinnertime conversation. Say: "How were the swings at the park today? Did you get a turn on the horsey swing?" Or: "What colors did you use for that drawing you did?"

Your child will have something to say. And then, at the end of dinner, *you* can say, "It was fun talking together tonight, wasn't it? I look forward to those times."

We tend to praise children when they come around to our way of thinking. It's good to compliment them at other times, too, just on general principle.

When you must take something away, offer a substitution in its place.

For the first two or three years of your child's life, you will often—*very* often—have to remove from her hands something she has or deny her something she desperately wants. She has no understanding of the danger or value of different items, of whom they belong to, of why the thing she wants is not possible or practical for her to have at the moment.

When you must take something away, offer something else in its place. She's in an exploring mood, and a very young child doesn't yet have the capacity to think of what else would satisfy her need for exploration at that moment. While she's still a baby, it may be fairly easy to redirect her attention—swap a plastic cup for the scissors she's picked up and chances are she'll contentedly bang her cup on a chair. When she gets a little older and knows she's not getting what she wants, you'll need to put more effort into the matter.

Nina Leif, in her wonderful books *The First Year of Life* and *The Second Year of Life,* describes this as a three-part process: First, limit the undesired behavior; second, offer a substitution; third, approve what the child is doing with the substitution.

Suppose your 2-year-old yanks out of your hands the magazine you've just started to read (and children absolutely *can't stand* seeing Mom sitting there reading by herself). Take the magazine back, and say: "This is Mommy's magazine. But look what's right over here, your Babar book. Let's look at your book together for a minute."

Help her turn a couple of pages. Ask her if she can open to the next page by herself. Say, "Good for you, the way you're turning those pages. Can you point to Babar's trunk? How about his tail? Good." Spend a little time helping her get engaged with this new activity. Say, "This is nice. We can sit here and both read—you look at your book and I'll look at my magazine."

The substitution of her book for your magazine may occupy her. Or it may not, and you'll have to put off your reading until you're able to enjoy a little private time at night. But you'll have a much greater chance of success if you help her get started and approve of what she's doing. A mother in one of my workshops said substitutions really started working once she added the "approving" part. It took about one quarter of the time to get her child redirected, she said, and the whole atmosphere was nicer.

As you limit her behavior and say "no," you teach your child important lessons: Some things are dangerous to play with and you're trying to keep her from hurting herself; some things belong to other people; she can, if she tries, overcome her disappointment and find other ways to play and explore.

As you offer a substitution at the same time, you not only

redirect her attention—you encourage her to keep exploring. The fact is that desire to grab, touch, manipulate, and have things is good and healthy and contributes to her intellectual growth. Your job: Make sure what she's grabbing, touching, holding is safe and appropriate.

And as you approve the new behavior, you're giving a "yes." That encourages her to repeat the desirable behavior and helps her feel competent.

The payoff is, by the time she reaches age 3 or 4 or 5, she may be able to start to find substitutions for herself.

Billy, 4½, loved his toy *Star Wars* sword. One day his friend came over for an afternoon; before long the sword was out, the two playmates became overexcited, the friend got poked, and both boys were unhappy *and* in danger of being hurt.

The little boy's father said: "Billy, we're going to have to put your sword away for now. You can see that it's not a good idea to play with it." Billy reluctantly handed Dad the sword, and then went running into his room to get his collection of action figures down from the shelf. He and his pal settled into a still lively but more peaceable game of good guy/bad guy space invaders.

In the next chapter, you'll see lots of examples of offering substitutions that work.

> Moments of change in the course of a day—
> leaving the house in the morning, for
> example—are hard for your child. Provide
> transitions to ease her through them.

A 3- or 4-year-old hates to call it quits to something that's fun—playing with her friend, for example, or watching her favorite Barney video. She doesn't see *why* she has to end the play date and go home or turn off the TV and come in to dinner.

In Chapter 4, I'll talk about some common situations in which children typically resist leaving the fun stuff, and how giving a 10- or 15-minute warning or other simple transition can help move things along.

But two points of change in the course of the day can be especially troublesome.

So many parents in my workshops say that the worst times with their children—the times of the most dawdling, power struggles, tantrums, and nagging—come in the morning, with trying to get out the door, and in the evening, with trying to call an end to the day. (Mornings, of course, are also when you feel most rushed; evenings, when you're tired and most desperately in need of a little time for yourself.)

You'll decrease the stalling or tantrums if you provide transitions. Here's why they work:

Young children are still *not absolutely sure* if or when they will come back to what they are leaving. They often have trouble separating from what's secure. Your youngster may absolutely adore preschool, but still be fearful or unhappy about leaving home to get there, and so she'll balk at coming in to breakfast or refuse to put on her shoes. It's just too hard to get up, get dressed, and go out the door.

Figure out a way to give your child a transition. Wake up earlier, and read or work a puzzle together, for that 20 minutes of uninterrupted, "on her turf" time I talked about earlier. If that's not possible, just have her nearby while you're getting dressed or shaving, and tell her what you're going to be doing during the day and what neat things she'll be doing at preschool or at the sitter's.

If she gets that transition time with you—and reminders that her next activity is going to be fun and worth the effort of getting ready to go out—chances are she'll be much more capable of leaving.

At night, if it's really, really hard for her to let go of rearranging her stuffed bears and get to bed, she may, like many children, have some fears about going to sleep. Or she may just realize there's so much to do while she's awake! Give her another reassuring transition.

Spend 5 or 10 minutes admiring her bears, and let her know that they'll stay there, undisturbed, available for her to play with tomorrow. Tell her that after the bedtime story and the good-night kiss and the lights-out, you'll come back in 10 minutes to look in on her and make sure she's all right.

Transitions don't take a lot of time; they can work wonders.

Praise your child—at the right time, with descriptive words, in the right amounts.

I meet many mothers and fathers who, reflecting on their childhoods, find their own parents were short on praise. Keeping toys picked up or being nice to a kid brother or, later on, getting good report cards was no more than what was expected. Nobody gave them many pats on the back for what they did appropriately or well. Others were praised, but only when they really excelled at something or for major accomplishments. As a result, they felt deficient a lot of the time.

Those same mothers and fathers very often feel they want to be more complimentary to their own kids. They think it is kinder and more loving, and they believe it promotes a child's confidence and self-esteem. With those admirable intentions, some tend to shower their youngster with big praise for every small thing he does.

It is *good* to applaud your child's *efforts* to learn new skills. Just think of all he's struggling to master during these first years, and how hard it is—to give up his nice, comforting bottle and drink milk and juice out of a cup that's so hard to hold on to; to get to the bathroom and pull his pants down and sit on the potty in time; to get the round block down the round hole and the square block down the square hole; to hold a crayon and draw a face on a piece of paper. He has to struggle through all this, get frustrated, keep on trying, and eventually get it done. That's how he achieves real confidence.

Your child will be warmed and encouraged when you praise his efforts—but the key word is *efforts*. And the key concept, when you admire his efforts, is to be *descriptive*.

Effective praise is descriptive. It lets a child understand what he did or accomplished so that he can reproduce the action or repeat the behavior another time. If you said to a friend, "You look great," she'd be pleased—and she might guess that you think her teal blue blouse and silver necklace are especially becoming to her. If you said, "That blue color is beautiful with your complexion and the necklace really sets off the cut of that blouse," she'd be clear about what you meant; she wouldn't have to guess.

Your child can't guess what you mean; he doesn't have enough experience. To a young child, you might describe his accomplishment like this: "You have a firm hold on your cup." Or "All your juice went in your mouth, you're really learning how to feed yourself." Or "You are really working hard on that drawing. I like the way you made the man's hair all big and bushy." That's good, descriptive praise.

Not-so-good praise is saying: "I'm so proud of my big, grown-up boy! You don't need that old baby bottle anymore." Or "That's the most beautiful picture! You're going to be Daddy's little artist."

As he gets a little older, you can combine praising his efforts with some constructive criticism and help. You might say: "Good for you, you got your shoes on and your laces started. Pretty soon you'll be tying your shoelaces all by yourself! While you're still practicing, if you do it a little more slowly it usually will work better."

And as he gets older and his actions start to resemble more adultlike behavior, don't forget the praise. When he walks down the street and waits for you at the crossing, for example, you might say, "It makes me feel so safe when I know you'll stop at the curb." Or "Putting napkins on the table and clearing off your dish helps us have more time for talking or reading."

Even young children come to know when praise is real and when it's exaggerated. As soon as your child starts spending regular time with his peers, with preschool teachers and generally in the bigger world outside his family, he learns very quickly that he isn't the best at everything and that everything he does isn't great. That is a lesson he has to learn on his road to independence. But he can handle the corrections and criticism much better when he has a whole memory bank full of positive experiences.

Change "no" to "yes," by telling your child what she can do (will get) and when she can do it, and not what she can't do (won't get).

If you ran a tape recorder for twenty-four hours and captured one day's worth of dialogue between you and your child, and then sat in a quiet place and listened to it carefully, I think you would hear yourself making many remarks like these:

"No juice right now, sweetie. You're going to have dinner in a few minutes."

"Playtime's over, you have to take your bath now."

"I know you want me to take you and Jason to the zoo tomorrow, but we can't. Remember I told you we have to go to Grandma's? And you love going to Grandma's, don't you?"

"Nope, I said only two bedtime stories. It's getting late."

What you would hear are a lot of "no's."

Of course, as a parent you must dictate many of the details of your youngster's day, deny inappropriate requests or demands, keep things moving along by calling a halt to some actions and getting others started. But consider what it's like for your child to hear "no" so often. You'd feel frustrated and irritated if you were in her shoes. You can go to the refrigerator and have some juice whenever you feel like it; she can't.

Switch "no" to "yes" as often as you can—and once you start thinking about how to do it, you'll be pleasantly surprised at how easy it is:

"You want that juice because you're really getting hungry, aren't you? Let's get your dinner started right now."

"Yes, I know you want to play a little longer. Do you want some help getting your dinosaurs put away so they'll be all ready for you to play with tomorrow? Then you can take your bath."

"Yes! Let's you and me and Jason go to the zoo. Maybe we can get there when the seals are being fed. We'll do that on Friday, the day after tomorrow."

"You bet we'll read this book. Let's put it right on the top of your list for bedtime tomorrow."

It's a small flip—from "No, you can't do that," to "Yes, I know you want to do that. You will be able to do that later, and here's what you can do now." You may not get an immediate, positive response. Your child, no dummy, is quite aware that she's not getting what she wants when she wants it. She may still be angry or disappointed or demanding. But she will be much more likely to accept the inevitable without a major power struggle.

Here's an example:

Amelia, age 3, brother Ben, and their father had a regular Saturday afternoon routine. All three went to Ben's piano lesson and then went out for cider and doughnuts, Amelia's favorite treat. And almost every week there was a battle, because Amelia wanted the treat first. One week, her dad tried changing "no" to "yes."

He said: "Sweetie, I know how much you love that cider and doughnuts, and you can have that right after Ben's lesson." Amelia's response: "I want it right now!" Dad: "Yes, I know you want it right now. Right now what you can have is either some cereal or some fruit."

Amelia didn't look happy. After a few moments, she

walked over to her mom, folded her arms, and said: "Have some cereal! Now!" She got her cereal and later her cider and doughnuts, and the outburst lasted half the time it had in the past. After two more Saturdays of this routine, that small battle was over.

Empathize. Put yourself in your child's shoes. Offer him your regrets, for example, that he must do something he doesn't want to do.

The dictionary defines empathy this way: "The ability to share in another's emotions, thoughts, or feelings."

You say to your youngster: "I know you're really angry with me because I'm making you leave the playground. I don't blame you! I don't like it either when people boss me around." Or "I'm sorry we have to leave now and I feel really bad that you're so upset. I know you want to stay longer, but we do have to go home." That's showing empathy.

And your child, even if he remains under a black cloud, feels understood.

It's not always easy to be empathetic to your child, especially when he's being impossible. Or you can lose the feeling quickly! You've expressed your regrets, you've shown your child you know he's unhappy, and with good cause, about the turn of events—and now you think you are justified in getting on with correcting the difficult behavior.

Wait until later. You can't correct without first acknowledging your child's feelings, and allowing some time for that understanding to settle in. Imagine this scene: Your spouse reminds you that the car needs gas, but you forget to stop at the station, the car goes bone dry along an empty stretch of highway, and you spend a stressful half an hour getting help. That evening, you relate this incident to your spouse, who says,

"Oh, that's awful. You must have been really upset. I'm sorry you had to go through that on your own, honey," and gives you a comforting hug. The next evening he says, "You know, I did tell you twice that you had to gas up the car. You really should have remembered." Wouldn't you feel more disposed to accept that criticism, now that your mate had the sense, grace or compassion to acknowledge your feelings first?

Empathy is a wonderful tool when sibling squabbles are making life unhappy for everybody. If your 4½-year-old seems to be in a perpetual, ill-spirited funk now that there's a younger brother constantly underfoot, imagine how he feels and what he's missing and then talk to him about it. You might say: "I know how hard it is for you to share everything with Matthew. We used to have a lot more time for the two of us to read and do things together. I miss that too. We have to find a way to get some more time for just you and me." Your child becomes aware that you know how he feels, and that you're missing him too. And then if you do come up with a plan for more time together and stick to it, suddenly he doesn't feel as jealous of his younger sibling.

Being empathetic can also involve sharing some of your own feelings and experiences. Let your child know that you, too, sometimes absolutely hate having to go to the store, and you help yourself snap out of that "I don't want to" feeling by thinking of some nice things that might happen along the way. Then maybe he can try that too.

A little empathy goes a long way.

> **Wait until the emotions (yours and hers) have settled before you try to correct behavior.**

Three-year-old Kami loved climbing up the steps on the big kid's slide at the playground. Kami and her mother had agreed that the little girl would go up as high as four steps and then come back down. But Kami's need to climb overcame her wish to stick by the rules and her desire not to get hurt, and one day she kept going up and up, despite her mom's entreaties to stop. The worried mother finally bribed her daughter down with a lollipop, then angrily took her straight home. Later, Kami's mother felt she hadn't handled the situation well.

Enticing the girl to come down with a treat and then dragging her home in anger maybe weren't the *ideal* responses; at the time, however, they were the best that mother could do.

When a lot is going on—when your child is getting overexcited and running wild or creating a public scene to end all scenes, when you have good reason to be worried for her safety or furious at her actions—don't expect to be able to act in a calm, cool, and collected manner. And don't expect to correct the misbehavior on the spot.

On such occasions, tempting a child into temporary obedience or picking her up and just getting the both of you out of there may not be a bad idea.

After the emotions, yours and hers, have died down, then you can think of ways to impose consequences and to set limits.

The next time Kami and her mother head for the park, Mom might say:

"I was very worried yesterday when you went so high and didn't come down when I told you to, and I got angry because I thought I could trust you to go only as far as we said. I know it's just so exciting for you right now to climb that ladder. But it's dangerous to go so high, so today when you want to climb I'm going to hold your hand. We're going to do that for a few times, and eventually you'll be able to go up there by yourself."

After the fact is also when you'll have most success getting your 3-, 4-, or 5-year-old involved in helping you find a solution. She, too, really doesn't want a repeat of yesterday's disastrous play date or last week's temper tantrum in the supermarket, and if you ask her what you both might do next time to make things better, she may come up with some good ideas.

> **Give your child hope. Let him know that what's not available to him right now or today or this year will be, somewhere down the road.**

Walking to school together, a father and his 5-year-old son came to a corner, where the little boy announced that he wanted to cross the street on his own and walk the rest of the way to school on his own. His father said, "No, you have to hold my hand."

That father was right to see first of all to his child's safety. But he might have done that *and* given his son a little hope for the future. He might have said something like this: "You know, I want you to be able to cross the street on your own. Not only that, I want you to be able to walk to school all by yourself. And that's exactly what I'm going to show you how to do, and by the time you're ten you'll be able to cross alone. We'll start practicing together right now, so you'll know how to do it when the time comes."

And then on their morning walks to school Dad might set up various ways to practice. As long as he stops at the corner, the little boy might be allowed to walk a few steps ahead of his father and pretend that Dad isn't there. At the corner, the little boy might say out loud what he has to do next—check the traffic light, look both ways, and so on.

Dad might point out to his son that one of the reasons he has to wait until he's older is that on streets where cars are parked along the side someone driving a car won't be able to see a little person who's trying to cross. And so the child gains some of his parent's perspective, and doesn't feel simply that he's being squelched in his wishes.

What's wonderful about giving your child hope in these little ways is this: Your youngster knows immediately that you genuinely want him to be independent. He takes heart because there's a time frame in mind—not only is he going to get to do what he wants, but he knows *when* that's going to happen—when you'll say "yes." And he can start working on it right now, and you'll teach him the steps so that he can get there.

In the next section of this book, you will be amazed, I think, to see how easy and how useful this tool is in all kinds of situations—not only when you must stop your child from doing something potentially dangerous, but when you want to impose consequences or show him that tomorrow's another day and you're not giving up on him!

Give your child hope, and he doesn't have to keep after you to get what he wants. Give him hope, and you'll reduce the nagging manyfold.

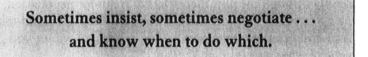

**Sometimes insist, sometimes negotiate . . .
and know when to do which.**

When it comes to matters of health, safety, and the law, you're the boss. The dictator, in fact. There can be no bargaining or meeting halfway about whether or not your youngster gets strapped into the car seat that she hates or holds your hand crossing the street or stops biting her friend.

There *can* be some discussion about *why* those actions have to happen: "Because riding in a car seat is the law . . . Because I have to make sure you don't get hit by a bus when we cross the street . . . Because you're not allowed to hurt people." There can't be discussion about *whether or not* they will happen.

You must also insist when it comes to being considerate of others. Since children under 3 aren't mature enough to think about others, parents have to keep their expectations at a minimum and lend a helping hand while kids are developing this ability. After age 3, a child begins to understand the effect of her behavior on others, and you can expect her to be more accountable.

Suppose Grandma is staying with you for a week and needs a nap every afternoon. Your 2½- and 4-year-olds are home from nursery school, it's raining outside, and you can't take them to the park to ensure an hour of quiet in the house.

Tell your children that Grandma needs to have them use their "inside voices" for the next hour. You can say you realize that's difficult to do, but you've planned some activities for them that will make it easier. And also tell them that Grandma will really appreciate their efforts and will be able to play with them when she's up. Since your 2½-year-old doesn't understand "an hour," explain that after he's played with the blocks, drawn a picture, and had a story and snack, he can start using his kiddie car again and he can use a louder voice.

Insist when you must insist. For the rest of the business of getting through the day, there's lots of room for negotiation, or trying to reach an agreement through a little give-and-take. Your child can get some of what she needs and wants; you get some of what you need and want.

Many of the tools in this chapter are all about negotiating— offering your child choices and substitutions, involving her in solutions to problems, helping her save face. Negotiating comes into play when your youngster protests leaving her friend's house, dawdles about putting on clothes in the morning, won't share her toys, and in so many other minor and major hassles.

Here are two truths about negotiating:

First, it works. All your child's most difficult behavior stems from growth, from her move toward independence. The more she senses that you appreciate her needs, that you're on her side, and that you're willing to work with her to help her get where she wants to be, the more cooperation you will gain—and the more easily, more pleasantly it will come.

Second, negotiating is hard! It's time-consuming! Most of us would rather not be bothered, especially since in most households with young children time is what you don't have much of. We just want our child to do what we want her to do. That certainly seems reasonable, since as loving parents we do know what's right and best for our children. Often, we just don't feel like negotiating or see why on earth we should have to.

A mother in one of my workshops said: "I can hardly believe how much work this is! It is a gigantic effort for me not to start yelling or nagging or threatening." There was a chorus of agreement from other parents in the room.

Then she added more. Just thinking about the tools, she said, and remembering to use them—to say to her son, for example, "I know you don't want to quit playing right now, you're having so much fun"—made her slow down, cool off, and think of a better solution than nagging and yelling. And she got better results.

Other parents had the same experiences:

"It's the pause, the time between the feeling and the action," said one, "that lets me think."

Said another: "I've got to tell you, this *is* a lot of work! But it's been gratifying, because I've seen changes. My daughter seems easier to get along with and even a little bit happier." That parent also feels more competent.

Most encounters in life involve negotiations, after all. I don't know anybody who just comes along and says sure to all your requests. You'll put in the time and energy to work out compromises with your spouse. Do the same for your child.

Ask your child what <u>she</u> thinks should be done to correct a behavior problem. Get her involved in the solution.

You've arrived at your friend's house to collect your child at the end of a scheduled play date, and as the minutes drag on, your daughter shows no signs of being willing to head for the door. You've been empathetic, you've told her that you know she's having so much fun, it's hard for her to leave. You're getting nowhere.

Instead of issuing one final, no-more-nonsense command, repeat the fact—"We have to get on our coats now and go home"—and then ask: "What do you think we should do here? What would make it easier for you to leave?"

You're letting your child know that there will be no more negotiating the fact, and she really is going to be out of there shortly, but you are willing to listen to any thoughts she has on how you both might get that accomplished. And then she just may think for a moment and ask if Jimmy can come over to her house to play next week. You say, "Absolutely. We'll make that date." She gets her coat, and off you go.

She's been involved in the solution of a problem. She's able to cooperate.

Asking your child what she would do to help solve a problem she's having is enormously effective when you are working on prevention of future misbehavior. If you spent all afternoon breaking up fistfights between your child and her playmate, that evening you might say: "That wasn't much fun today, was it? What can we do next time you get together so you'll have more fun? Let me give you some ideas, and you see what you think. Would you like me to stay in the room with both of you? Should we get some better snacks to eat?" Children younger than age 3 usually can't think of solutions; you'll have to come up with some. Older kids will have their own suggestions.

Getting your child involved in solutions is going to be one of your most powerful tools for years to come, right up until the time your teenage son or daughter heads off for college. Whether the problem has to do with refusing to put on shoes in the morning or eat dinner at night, with difficulty playing nicely or settling down to homework, the more a child is encouraged to participate in a solution, the more successful that solution will be.

Children who come up with their own ideas on how to get

themselves behaving better tend to follow their own decisions. And they feel good about themselves.

Ask your child for solutions, and her sense of competence and self-esteem rises. You're setting limits, you're letting her know this can't go on or can't be this way next time, but you're also saying you respect her enough to include her in improving the picture.

Your child will like the idea that she can make things better. Your confidence that she can appeals to her sense of capability.

> ## Grab your child, if you must—and sometimes you must—but don't slap.

"I never really hit my son," said a mother in one of my groups. "I do give him a smack on the rear occasionally. It's the only way to get his attention or to get him to stop doing something."

I know what that mother is feeling. I'm sure you do too. You've asked your youngster five times, nicely, to stop throwing his toy spacemen wildly around the room or to quit tormenting his little sister. No reaction. Then matters go from annoying to raucous to worse, and your child's play date pal gets bonked in the head or his little sister is in tears. Suddenly, you've had as much of this as you want to take. You're thinking, "I've been reasonable and nice, why can't I get a little cooperation here?" And you dash in and give your child a quick swat on the seat of his overalls to put an end to it.

Here's another kind of occasion when a parent almost instinctively is inclined to slap: You're walking along holding your toddler's hand, and he wrenches free, dashes off, and heads straight for the street. You race after him (horrified that your giving chase is now causing him to laugh and run away even faster), catch him by the arm just as he reaches the curb, and administer a sound thwack on the rear.

Almost always, a parent slaps out of worry that the child is in immediate danger, or out of frustration or impatience, because the parent wants and expects the youngster to learn more quickly.

Many parents see nothing wrong with those smacks. Many others blame themselves harshly—I've known mothers who, years after the fact, still vividly remember and regret the *one time* they hit their child, and wish they could take it back.

Don't worry too much about any lasting damage being done from the occasional slap. *But try not to slap at all.*

Slapping or hitting teaches a child that it's all right to settle problems with hands rather than with words. And children, always, will do what we do, learn their lessons from our behavior. You don't want to teach your child that physical force is acceptable. You *do* want to help him learn to cool off, get control, and use words—yelling them if necessary!—to let others know he doesn't like something.

Demonstrate those lessons yourself. When your youngster really does need to comply with your wishes, get down at his level, grab him firmly by the wrists or shoulders, look him in the eye, and say: "I mean business! I've told you what I expect you to do. Now just sit there, cool down, and then get started on it." If he won't meet your eyes, say: "I'd prefer that you look at me, but you can look away if you want. But you must understand that I mean business here!"

Follow that tactic when you must snatch your child back from the street corner. Maybe out of your fear, you'll shout and yell. Later, you might want to explain and apologize to your child. Say: "Look, when you go dashing off like that and you're in danger of getting hurt, I'm going to be very upset and I'm going to act in ways that neither of us likes. But we cannot have you get hurt."

Without hitting, you can be stern, you can even be *physical*— a really firm grasp of the wrists or shoulders (no shaking) will be felt by your child.

Grab, don't slap.

> ## Give reasonable consequences for misbehavior.

A mother and father and their 4-year-old son went out for a Friday evening dinner. Zack was excited about going to a grown-up restaurant with his mom and dad, and all went well—at first. Soon his excitement got the better of him, and Zack was dumping the salt shaker contents over the table, jumping off his chair to run around, and generally, his father said, "acting like a holy terror." When no distractions, including a break to walk around outside, settled him down, his parents cut the evening short.

A week later, they tried again, first telling Zack they would get to the restaurant earlier so they wouldn't have to wait too long for their food and they'd bring crayons and paper so he could draw at the table. But the same unhappy scene occurred.

The next day, Zack's father said to his son: "Zack, it looks like you're not really ready to go out for dinner with Mom and me. The next couple of times we go out it would be better for you to stay home with the baby-sitter. It's just too tough for you right now to sit quietly with us at the restaurant, but I know you'll be able to do that when you're a little older and we'll try again in a while."

Zack protested mightily—he really loved those evenings out. But his parents held firm.

That was an appropriate consequence for the fact that Zack made it unpleasant for everybody at the restaurant. It came coupled with expressions of empathy ("I know this is hard for you right now") and hope for the future ("You'll be able to handle this someday").

It was not a punishment. Parents who punish a child have the idea they need to "teach the kid a lesson" through some form of fear, threat, humiliation, or—as with spanking—pain or discomfort. That parent may achieve some momentary compliance, but the child tends to forget what he did wrong and is much more interested in getting even with Mom or Dad!

Good consequences make sense in terms of the offense. Almost always, they involve the suspension of a privilege. Ideally, as with Zack's losing the privilege of going out with his parents, the consequences will be related to the misbehavior.

Some consequences you will use on the spot to try to correct a misbehavior: If your 3-year-old can't stop punching and hitting her playmate, send her to the living room couch for a short time-out, with the promise that she can try again later. Since hitting and punching aren't allowed, she loses the privilege of playing for the space of a time-out.

Some consequences you'll use ahead of time to try to prevent a repeat of the trouble or promote a little greater cooperation. If for two afternoons in a row your child has been punching and hitting her playmate, on the third day you might say: "You know, it's been very hard for you not to start a fight with Jessie lately, so we're not going to ask her over to play for a little while. We're going to give it a rest, and maybe we can try a play date again next week."

At the same time, use some of your other tools—ask your child what she thinks you all might do to make things go more smoothly next time, or offer some suggestions of your own; let her know you're absolutely sure she *will* be able to get control of this punching and hitting; on the next go-round, spend a few more minutes being a play date supervisor.

A good consequence given in a respectful manner sets limits and conveys a firm message. You're saying, This is unacceptable behavior and I won't allow it to continue right now or to happen again.

It probably *will* happen again—your child doesn't grow that fast!—but with your empathetic support along the way, she'll get there.

> **Let your child know his behavior has an impact on you or others. Tell him something he said or did hurt your feelings or made you happy.**

A very young child doesn't instinctively understand that what he does affects other people. He does *need* to learn that truth, because it's a key to his moral development and to his growth as an empathetic, sensitive, and caring individual.

You help him along in that process by letting him know when his actions have some fallout on the people around him.

If his toys are strewn about the living room and he's making no move to comply with your request that he pick them up, you might say: "Listen, these things do have to be put away because it's hard to walk through here, and somebody might trip over those blocks."

If your child gives a shove to the lady walking in front of him into the bus because he's in a rush to get to the backseat, suggest he apologize. Later, tell him: "When you push somebody, that person doesn't like it. You should say you're sorry. That will make the person feel better."

If your little boy shouts, "You're an old dummyhead, Daddy," you might say: "I don't like hearing that. It hurts my feelings. And you know what? I don't feel like playing with you when you call me that."

If your youngster has a nice chat on the phone with his grandmother, tell him the next day: "I talked to Nana this morning, and she told me she loved talking to you last night. She really likes hearing about your art projects."

If he's been able to share a favorite toy or go along with his friend's desire to play a different game, let him know you were happy he could do that, because you know it wasn't so easy, and his friend looked happy too.

Every time you talk to him, without gushing or without scolding, about the good or the not-so-good behaviors, you're helping him see that his actions have an effect on other people. That's a lesson he's learning pretty well by ages 3 and 4; certainly by that time he should be expected to take steps to correct something he's done wrong, by an apology or, more important, by making amends. If, for example, he's spilled crackers all over the floor, he needs to clean them up. Tell him, "Crumbs are bad for the rug and the mess keeps others from enjoying the living room."

When he's a little older—even between 4 and 5—he can work on it some more. If his playmate is in the playground looking unhappy, you can ask your child: "What do you think Jeremy needs right now? Can you do anything to make him feel better?" And you and your youngster might figure out that Jeremy doesn't like his baby sister, and he might enjoy being invited over for a long play date. Afterward, help your child appreciate what happened: Jeremy had a great time and seemed happier.

Parents these days have been so indoctrinated to the importance of building a child's self-esteem. They rush to forgive and reassure a child after he's done something wrong, because they're trying to make him feel good about himself. But real self-esteem comes in part from acting thoughtfully and responsibly to other people. That's why we have to teach kids that what they do, good or bad, has an effect on others.

> **Let your child know what's coming next.
> When he knows what to expect and begins
> to learn to anticipate events, he's less likely
> to be upset or whiny.**

It's difficult for us adults to appreciate how powerfully young children *don't* know what's coming next, and how uncomfortable that can be for them.

By the time your youngster is about 8 or 9 months old, he does expect and trust you to feed him. He knows you regularly take away his hunger and he's also become familiar with the sounds of food preparation, so if you have him propped up in his infant seat near you in the kitchen, he probably won't fuss and cry while he's waiting for dinner.

Over the next several years, his capacity to anticipate events grows, and along with it comes a greater ability to delay gratification. It's a slow process. The better you are at anticipating his needs, the better that process will go.

One way to anticipate his needs is to give him attention before he's desperate for it. Often, your toddler will nag at you because he doesn't really know *when* you're going to be available to him again. He doesn't know what to expect.

One mother wanted to spend a Sunday afternoon working on a home repair project with her husband. Before doing that, she devoted an hour to her young son. They played trains, built blocks, and had a wonderful time. And when she went off to do her own thing, her little boy was content to play by himself for over an hour and a half. When he did come back for some more attention, it wasn't in a demanding way. He had been filled up, and so he didn't have to complain.

Telling a child what to expect also helps children under the age of 3 cooperate more, since they only have a time sense of "now" and some understanding of "soon." By describing to your child that one activity follows another, you help him learn to judge time *and* wait for an activity or event. If he's eager for his play date and asking, "When is Justin coming? When is Justin coming?" telling him "in two hours" won't give him much help. He's more likely to settle down if you say: "First, we'll have breakfast, then get dressed, then we can play blocks, pick up the blocks, and after that you'll see Justin."

As he grows older, help your child anticipate events. Give him a short-term and long-term perspective—what's going to happen soon and what's going to happen down the road. It puts an order to his life; it helps him learn to tell time; it helps him feel safe. And it can work small wonders in cutting down on daily fussing, dawdling, and misbehaving.

If you know tomorrow morning is going to be hectic, for example, tell your youngster tonight: "We're going to be very busy tomorrow because we have to drop Roger at the vet before we go to play group and we have to bring the cupcakes and hats for your party. I'm going to depend on you to come down for breakfast right on time, okay?" If you're in the car and you've got to concentrate, say: "Pretty soon we're going over the bridge, and I'll have to stop and pay the toll and then figure out what road we need to take. So no talking. You can listen to your tape, and soon I'll be able to talk to you again."

And whenever there's something a little out of the ordinary about to happen in your lives—say Mom is leaving on a three-day business trip—that's when it's especially important to tell your child what comes next, in *his* life. He doesn't want to know what *you'll* be doing. He wants to know: *What happens to me?* Tell him he and Dad will go to Grandma's for dinner on Friday, and later that evening they'll call Mom where she's staying and he can talk to her, and on Saturday Josh will come over to play . . . and so on.

When your child knows what to expect, he feels more in control. And then he's more willing to cooperate.

Give your child words to use.

Once your child has acquired a few skills, she's not going to fight with you so much. It makes sense: When she can get her pants and sweater on by herself, feed herself, open doors by herself, she's no longer so inclined to run off down the street or shout "No, no, no!" in an effort to discharge frustration and assert independence.

One of the biggest skills, of course, is language. Toddlers have a lot of desires but not a lot of language, and that's what produces much of the aggressive behavior between playmates and in preschool groups.

Your 2½-year-old wants the toy her friend is playing with, so she goes over and yanks it out of the friend's hands. The friend starts to cry or, just as likely, gives a shove and yanks the toy back. This is fairly standard toddler behavior, but you can help your child learn words to use instead: "When you want something your friend has, say, 'I want to play with that now.' " She may not *get* what she wants just when she wants it, but you're building up her language skills, letting her know it's right to ask for things rather than grab them, and setting the stage for later lessons in taking turns.

Jamie and her pal Molly played together happily until Molly acquired a baby brother, which didn't please her. Suddenly when Molly came over to play she was pushing and hitting Jamie and taking her toys away. Jamie and her mother talked this over, and Jamie's mom gave her words to use: "If this happens again, you can say to Molly, 'If you're going to hit, you have to go home.' " They followed through; at the next two play dates, Jamie and her mother took Molly home early, before she wanted to leave. After that, the shoving and hitting stopped. The words empowered Jamie.

A quiet child who'd like to join in the group's activities but doesn't know how and always ends up on the sidelines can use some words. Tell her: "When you want to play with the others, you can say, 'I want to do that, too, can I help you?' Or you can say, 'I'm going to use the scooper while you use the frying pan, okay?' " When she has some suggestions on what to say, she just might feel a little surge of confidence in the social arena.

There's another way to give your child words to use. Put words to her feelings. A young child can be very upset by her own intense emotions. When you say, simply, "You're really sad today, aren't you?" or "You were so angry with me before" or "I bet you're feeling very excited and also kind of scared about staying over at Emma's house tonight," you give your child a lot of help.

You label something that may seem to her overwhelming or indescribable; you let her know that since it has a label everybody must have that feeling sometimes; you guide her along toward a vocabulary that she can use to describe what's on her mind or in her heart.

> **Be your child's play date supervisor. She needs help in learning how to be with other children.**

Play is a child's work. You've heard that before, and perhaps it sounded like an awfully serious notion. But when you think of the "work" your youngster accomplishes during the first five years of her life—learning language and social skills, trying out ideas about how the world works, dealing with anger and fears and other emotions—it's clear that she gets a lot of that done through playing. And play, which can go any way she wants it to go, is freeing and fun.

While your child is still an infant, you'll be initiating a lot of the play, with peekaboo and this-little-piggy-went-to-market games. As she grows through toddlerhood and the preschool years, her playing becomes richer and more complex, and involves other kids. Here's where a lot of parents I talk to run into difficulties.

First, they think two youngsters—provided with lots of playthings and a safe environment—should be left alone to develop their own games and work out their own differences, because that's how children learn important lessons about cooperation and taking turns. Second, they become very upset when those two kids *can't* work out their differences, at least without pushing, hitting, grabbing, and many tears, and that's when Mom, Dad, or the sitter comes on the scene to urge the children to share.

Those parental inclinations aren't entirely wrong. Your child and her little friend need to be given the freedom to make their own fun and games. But especially between the ages of about 1½ and 3 years, your child will benefit and learn better if you stand ready to be a supervisor during play dates.

Here are some ideas to keep in mind:

Letting youngsters "argue it out" over an activity or toy isn't a great idea, because one child usually dominates the situation and the other becomes the victim.

Sharing doesn't come naturally for toddlers. A child feels fiercely possessive of what is "mine." Her unwillingness to let another child use her stuff doesn't mean she's spoiled or selfish; those objects are an extension of herself.

When two youngsters are in a tussle over a particular plaything, usually you'll get nowhere if you ask, "Who had it first?" or "Whose turn is it now?" They don't know or can't give you a straight answer. Offer distractions—a snack or a new game to play—or your own solutions (they won't have their own) to how they might both use the object in dispute.

Toddlers find it easier to share when there are lots of a particular plaything—books or blocks, for example. Your child may find it *impossible* to share any item that is very special and precious and one-of-a-kind to her. Put those things up in the closet before a play date; she shouldn't have to share them.

If you've learned from past experience that your child and the particular friend who's coming over for a play date always end up in arguments over who gets to do what, see if you can plan ahead of time some activities in which they will have to work together—maybe making a giant necklace by both stringing wooden beads from opposite ends.

Sometimes one child becomes unhappy not because she wants the particular item that her friend is using, but because she wants to join in the friend's activity and doesn't know how. If one is having great fun draping old neckties around her stuffed bear, get out some more ties and the stuffed panda for the other to use.

Remember that this is when you're giving your child words to use. As a play date supervisor, you'll see many opportunities to remind her: "No hitting. Ask Emma if you can use that now."

> **When you can, appoint a neutral bad guy (blame it on the weatherman).**

A mother in one of my workshops dreaded cold fall and winter mornings. Martin, her 4-year-old, hated bundling up in sweater, coat, hat, and gloves, and forget about boots. Getting out the door to school never happened without Mom nagging and, often, forcibly dressing her child. One day, she came up with this clever tactic:

On a long sheet of paper she wrote 20, 30, 40, 50, 60, 70, and next to each number, drew a little picture of a child wearing different items of clothing according to the temperature. At 70 degrees, the little figure had on shorts and a T-shirt (the ideal outfit for any day of the year, according to her son); at 40 degrees, it wore a green hooded jacket (just like Martin's) and a wool scarf; by 20 degrees, the works—hat, gloves, parka.

Each morning, Martin and his mom would listen to the weather report on the radio, get the temperature, and check the chart to see what clothing had to go on that day. The protests, yelling, and nagging subsided.

Getting dressed appropriately is a major battleground for many parents and little kids, and in a later section we'll talk about several ways a parent might negotiate this particular issue. I like Martin's mother's solution, because it shows how really useful it can be at times to let somebody else besides the parent be the authority figure.

You have probably noticed that your child's preschool teacher or the nurse in the pediatrician's office or even your next-door neighbor can elicit your child's compliance in small matters far more easily than you can! That's because you're the person your child, on his road to independence, must push off against and resist. When you can, make life easier on yourself by appointing a neutral bad guy.

If, for example, your youngster hates getting buckled up in his car seat belt, say: "I know you don't like being in that seat belt, but I want you to be safe in the car. And besides that, it's the law that we have to wear seat belts. If you don't, Mommy can be pulled to the side of the road by a policeman and given a fine, because this is the law. We can stop later on and get out so you can walk around a little."

This is using an authority figure in a nonthreatening way.

A friend told me this incident, from a time when she was about 10 and her sister was about 5. One night, as the two girls were horsing around in their bedroom, her little sister ripped off the mattress tag that said, "Don't remove this tag under penalty of the law," or some such wording. Teasing, she told her sister that the mattress police would come after her, and for days afterward the little girl was nervously waiting for two policemen to show up at the front door and tell her parents what she had done.

The two sisters laugh about it now, but it wasn't funny for the little girl back then. It's never good to threaten a child with punishment from an outside authority figure. It's perfectly all right—and useful—to call on another voice of authority besides your own, and let your child know that those people are also looking out for his welfare, are there to help him stay warm or healthy or safe.

Set up success stories, opportunities for your child to do a small thing well to contribute to the smooth running of the family.

Most thoughtful parents take care to help a child feel successful at something he's trying to do. If he's frustrated and angry with himself because he can't get any of the parts in his eight-piece jigsaw puzzle to fit right, Mom or Dad will guide his hand to put six parts in place and then applaud him as he figures out the last two by himself. They seek to build his self-esteem by helping him achieve little successes when and where he can.

Sometimes, those same parents might overlook another way to help a youngster feel good about himself. Give your child chances to be competent within the family, so he benefits from knowing he's an important member of this group of people he's living with.

Many parents, I find, know it's good to teach a child to be responsible for his own possessions. They will remind him to put his dirty clothes in the laundry basket and pick up his toys at the end of the day. This is all to the good. But it's also good to broaden the range of your child's participation. Just to take care of yourself isn't enough in the long run, after all—it's a start, but it's not enough.

In farm families, in former times and still today, even very young children are put to work for the necessary functioning of the family, and they feel useful because of it. But most of our children aren't needed in those ways and so don't have the opportunity to feel significant because of them. Especially in small families, children are given few tasks. (Studies show that the more children in a household, the more each is expected to do. Only children have the fewest chores of all!)

Set up small chores that your child can handle and will be expected to do on a regular basis. Maybe he can fold the napkins for dinner each evening or put forks on the table, scrape the plates into the garbage, fill up the cat's food dish each morning, help unpack groceries. Change the chores every couple of weeks so they don't get boring and therefore cause a rebellion.

Children feel better about themselves and tend to be more cooperative if they think they have an important place in the household. They like the sense of contributing to the betterment and smooth running of the family. And most of us parents want our kids to see beyond themselves. That, after all, is what produces a moral child.

> **Kids have their pride. Let your child save face; sometimes she'll cooperate in a flash if she can just get in the last word.**

Five-year-old Zoe was three months into kindergarten at a small, private girls' school when she began to balk each morning at putting on the jumper and blouse that were the required dress. Her parents were getting fed up with the daily hassles. One morning Zoe announced that she didn't have to wear her uniform that day. Her mom said: "Are you sure?" Zoe: "Yes. Nobody has to wear the uniform today." Mom: "You're not going to wear your uniform and nobody else is either?" Zoe: "Right. No uniforms."

Zoe and her mother headed off, and as they arrived near school, both saw Zoe's little classmates, all in the required jumper and blouse. And suddenly Zoe wasn't feeling very well, she told her mom. She was too sick to go to school; couldn't they go home?

Zoe's mother said: "Well, it looks like everybody's wearing a uniform today after all. You know something? I thought that you might change your mind, and I brought your uniform along in this bag just in case. We can go in the bathroom if you want and put it on."

Zoe, overcome with relief, gave her mom a huge hug. Mother and daughter went in the bathroom and got Zoe changed, and uniform hassles didn't happen again.

That mother might have been tempted to give her daughter a taste of her own medicine, letting her experience the consequences of making up a story by being the only girl not dressed properly. But she chose a gentler approach. She recognized that Zoe was a generally respectful child who didn't make unwarranted protests and who just maybe, right at that point, was tired of all the rules at her new school and needed to make a statement and assert some control. And so Zoe's mother let her child save face. It's what I call a win-win situation.

When your child is being contrary or defiant or stubborn, it can be easy for you both to become backed into respective corners. She's digging in her heels, for any one of a host of reasons, against something she must do; you have been accommodating in the extreme, you think, and resent being pushed one more inch.

Often, that's just when one more inch will turn the tide. A young child who knows she's going to give in, who knows she's going to cooperate and go along with the program—because she has to and because, really, she wants to—may make one more, sometimes silly, sweet, small demand or push. As she does finally comply with your requests that she get ready to go with you to the store, she may say grumpily, "Okay, but I'm taking Big Bird along . . . you carry him." It's one more effort to get in the last word.

Let her have it. As she relinquishes a bit of independence, she's trying to save face.

In Chapter 4, you'll see how letting a child save face makes it easier for her to comply with your wishes and reduces the nagging. It's a way of showing respect for your child.

> **Learn to spot your own "I'm about to lose it" trigger points. Cool off in whatever way works for you—leave the room, take three deep breaths, do a little dance.**

Here's a scene witnessed by a mother in one of my workshops:

Two women were walking down a road in the local park, talking animatedly between themselves, as a 2-year-old boy ran about fifteen feet behind them. The boy was crying, obviously distressed about being unable to catch up to the two adults. After a bit, the women stopped and turned around, the boy reached them, one woman picked him up, spoke to him briefly and put him down again. Then the two adults resumed walking, and the little boy resumed running after them and crying frantically.

The parents in our group guessed the background to that scene, which the mother who saw it found distressing. The boy's mother had told him, not once but three or four or five times, that they needed to leave the benches or sandbox where they'd been resting, snacking, and playing, and head out of the park toward the car or home. He was having a great time where he was, and wanted no part of that plan. So Mom, disgusted, and her friend packed up and walked off, leaving the boy to follow.

We all said how frightened he must have felt when he realized he couldn't catch up. And by the time his mother stopped to pick him up, he was clearly too upset to be reassured, comfort himself, and calm down.

Then a father in the group sheepishly told a similar story. After a miserable, cranky Saturday morning with Alice, his 3-year-old, when they really *had* to leave the house on an errand, when Alice's protests had escalated to a full-blown tantrum, this dad said, "I'm leaving," put on his coat, and walked out the door. Alice ran screaming after him. The up-shot: Alice quieted down, let Dad put on his coat, and out they went on their errand. The problem was, Alice was fearful for some time after that about her father leaving her.

As parents, many of you have reached that point. Your patience is sapped, your anger is high, you lose it and act in a way you later wish you hadn't.

You don't want to resort to nagging and shouting, because that makes everyone feel bad and heightens the atmosphere of anger and tension. Even more important: You don't want to resort to any action—such as walking out, which suggests to your child you are abandoning him—that uses threats or fear to scare a youngster into acquiescence.

In the next chapter, you'll see several nicer, kinder ways Alice's mother could get her daughter's cooperation. And there's something else you can do to prevent an outburst you don't want. Learn to spot your own trigger points, and take a break before you lose it.

Go in your bedroom, close the door, and spend 5 minutes tidying up your desk or your sweater drawer.

Go in the kitchen, turn on some music, make a cup of tea (perhaps skip coffee—it frequently makes you more irritable).

Do whatever is your own most effective equivalent of counting to ten, cool off, and you'll be in a much better frame of mind to see how you might put to good use some of the other tools at your disposal.

And here's something else to remember: You're less likely to reach those trigger points in the first place if you regularly plan free time for yourself. Take an hour or two here and there to do something just for you. You'll return to your child calmer and refreshed; you'll do a more positive parenting job.

Model polite behavior to your child. Sometimes that means saying to him, "I'm sorry."

When *you* have behaved toward your child in a way that made you feel bad, when you've lost it and shouted or said something you regretted, apologize, on the spot or later. Your youngster sees that even *grown-ups,* even *parents,* get things wrong sometimes and then say they're sorry about it.

Three-year-old Jenny and her dad had agreed that Jenny could answer the phone one afternoon, then hand the phone to him; Dad was expecting a call from Jenny's aunt. When the phone rang, Jenny answered but refused to turn it over to her father. Finally, he grabbed the phone away angrily, and a little hitting and pushing contest between father and daughter followed.

After finishing his call, Jenny's father, calmed down by this time, said to his daughter: "I'm really sorry I did that. It wasn't right of me to grab the phone and to push you. But what you did really made me mad. We both have some progress to make. I promise I'll work harder on not getting so mad, and you can work harder on not trying to make me mad."

Later, Jenny said: "I get into trouble, Daddy, but I always love you." Dad said he always loved Jenny too.

Here's another example of a situation that might call for a well-timed apology:

You've just come in after a horrendous day at work, you're soaked from the rain, you couldn't get a cab, your mood is foul. Your child runs to you happily, grabs you around your very damp leg and won't let go, and you say, obvious annoyance in your voice: "Samantha, just leave me alone right now, okay? Go inside and play. I can't pick you up now." Samantha goes off dejectedly.

Foul days happen to us all. If you can go to your youngster and say: "Honey, I'm sorry I was in such a crabby mood. I had a terrible day and I needed a little time to myself. I shouldn't have acted mean, but it's not because of you," you both will feel better for it. (One day down the road she might just say to you, "You're being very grumpy and I know it's nothing I did. Did you have a bad day at work?" I know one little boy who did just that! When your child can be empathetic to you, you know you've been doing something right.)

More important, you're modeling polite behavior.

Sometime during the latter half of these first 5 years your child can begin to understand and often practice basic good manners, which have at their core respect for others. You help him learn about good manners and polite behavior when you demonstrate respect for him: Listen to him—really listen—while he's talking to you; introduce him to your friend you meet on the street; say please and thank you to him, family members, and others. And if you did something to him you didn't intend to do and you feel bad about it, say "I'm sorry."

> ## To defuse a problem instantly, backtrack.
> ## Say: "Let's start over again" or
> ## "Let's erase the blackboard."

This is a simple tool, for special occasions, that works like a charm.

Here's the occasion: You've been a veritable prince of a parent the whole day, spending lots of good time with your child. You've taken her on a long outing in the park, played puppets down on the floor, fixed her favorite snack of cheese and Cheerios. But she's having a cranky day and nothing much is satisfying her. There's been a minitantrum or two and a whole lot of whining.

You've pulled out all your tools. You have been empathetic (to a fault, you would say), offered choices, let her save face, given her hope that tomorrow things will go better. More sulks, more whining . . . until you're starting to feel up against a wall.

That evening, your child walks into the kitchen and starts complaining: "You said we could do Legos tonight. When are you going to play with me?" You (still reasonable) say: "I have to cook dinner now. You go in the other room and you can look at your book until I'm finished." She says: "I don't want to! Why do I have to do that?" Suddenly, you're yelling: "Look, you are not the only person in this household! I've been with you all day long, I have other things to do, I can't drop everything just because you want me to." You're into it now. You go back and forth, each getting whinier or madder.

This is when you backtrack. Stop and say: "Oops. We've got to start over again. Let's erase the blackboard." That will do it.

A mother in one of my workshops used this tool more than once with her very spirited 4-year-old. With a laugh, she told our group the following story. On one particular, seemingly endless day, not only was her daughter griping and demanding, she herself was fighting a killer headache. That evening, Mom went into her bedroom to lie down for a few minutes. Her daughter followed her in, with some added complaints. This mother shouted: "You have been making me miserable all day long! I can't stand to be in the same room with you right now! Leave! Leave!" Her daughter stared at her for a moment and then said: "Mommy, let's just erase the blackboard." Whereupon Mom stared at her child for a moment and then said: "You're right, honey. Let's erase the blackboard and start over again."

What goes around, comes around. It's a good tool for parent *and* child.

> **When your child is going through an impossible-to-live-with stage, find help! Farm her out for a weekend with the grandparents, hire baby-sitters, get your spouse more involved. You need a breather.**

The father of a 3½-year-old says his daughter recently turned from a little dream to a little nightmare. Mornings, when everyone is somewhat rested, run fairly smoothly, but life with Charlotte goes downhill after that. Dinnertime is a battle over whether she will or will not eat the prepared meal. Reading time is a battle over whether she will or will not get one more book read.

When Dad tells Charlotte it's time to brush her teeth and get ready for bed, this little girl doesn't just say, "I don't want to." She doesn't just quietly refuse to cooperate by continuing her coloring or castle-building. Charlotte shouts: "No! I won't!"

When Dad starts packing away the coloring book and crayons for the night, Charlotte flies into a rage. She throws herself on the floor, she screams, she kicks.

Charlotte's father pulled out all the tools, none of which made much of a dent with his impossible-to-live with, tantrum-throwing child. When Charlotte started to raise a ruckus, her father said calmly to his daughter, "I really don't want to listen to all this noise and crying," and went into his bedroom and closed the door.

After several weeks of such misery, Dad got a bright idea. He told his daughter that since they've been having a tough time in the evenings it would be better for both of them to have a sitter around dinner and bedtime for a while. He hired a teenage neighbor to baby-sit every evening. The baby-sitter took over, with much more success in leading Charlotte through the necessities of the rest of her day. (Kids generally find it easier to cooperate with someone other than a parent). Charlotte's father gave her a consequence, told her what to expect next (two other tools), and the sitter made all the difference in the world.

From time to time during your child's early years, you may, quite desperately, need to get away from her! Even sweet-natured children can go through impossible stages—typically, ages $2^3/4$, $3^1/2$, and $4^1/2$ are the pits.

It will end.

You're not doing anything wrong.

For a while, try to shift routine responsibilities to another caregiver. Not everyone can hire a baby-sitter on a regular basis, but perhaps you can ask your spouse to handle more of the child-raising duties. Maybe your sister would like to have her little niece spend a nice, long weekend at her house.

It doesn't mean you're a deficient parent if, for a brief interlude, you give yourself and your child some time off from each other.

> **Use a little humor, drama, or exaggeration to make a point. Sometimes go over the top; your child will be surprised and delighted.**

When nothing else seems to work, get theatrical to make your point. This is your opportunity to be an actor. As long as it doesn't come across as sarcasm or a put-down, a dramatic, exaggerated reaction will almost certainly grab your child's attention in a positive way.

If you've been after your youngster for the last three hours—with no success—to pick up his messy bedroom, stand in his doorway (wringing hands) and exclaim: "Oh, my goodness, how will I ever be able to get into this room? I've got it! I know! I'll go right now and put my boots on, so I'll be able to wade through this mess."

If you've called your child three times to announce that dinner is ready, say in a loud, pathetic voice: "Oh, I'm starving, I'm soooo hungry, I'm going to fall over from being so hungry, but Kurt won't come in to dinner. What am I going to do? What am I going to do?"

You get the idea. Especially if you and your child have been embroiled that day in more than the usual number of battles and defiances, switching gears this way can break the tension between the two of you. You take your child by surprise—this is not how he's expecting you to act!

Kids love it when parents can act funny or silly.

> **Plan joint approaches with your spouse.**

You and your spouse are not always going to be in agreement on parenting issues and approaches. You each bring to the business of being a parent your own family history, which may lead to feelings that you want to do things *very differently* from or *just like* your mother or father.

Most parents I meet want to be kinder and more democratic to their child than they feel their own parents were, and yet they sometimes still have trouble responding in those kinder, more democratic ways. There's a little voice saying: All this wasn't done for me, my parents weren't this accommodating, I survived, my child will have to too.

You and your spouse also may spend different kinds of time with your child or children. Maybe Mom is always the one who takes care of meals, baths, and doctors' appointments; Dad does preschool drop-offs and bedtime stories. One mother in my workshop said: "Women think of the house as an office and men think of it as a play yard." Each parent might get a slightly different version of the same child.

As much as possible, however, and *especially* when you're working at correcting a particular misbehavior, try to plan joint approaches.

If, for example, your 3-year-old daughter is currently pulling away from you on the street, and she and your spouse are heading out for Saturday morning in the park, tell your spouse what you've been doing to encourage holding hands. Help your spouse get the idea that you're trying not just to *stop* your child from doing something but to show her what she *can* do or *should* do.

And then, appreciate, enjoy, and *use* your different strengths or inclinations as parents. Allow for the complementary nature of your partnership.

Suppose that during that 20 minutes of child-directed playtime you've started, all your youngster wants to do is have Barbie dolls talk to each other in little squeaky voices, and after two days of this you're going up the wall. If you really hate playing talking Barbies and your spouse thinks it's fun, let your spouse do it.

One mother doesn't especially enjoy playground outings with her child, although she loves taking him on long stroller walks and visiting museums. Her husband, on the other hand, is happy passing leisurely weekend afternoons in the playground with their toddler, and so he does. "He's the perfect park bench parent," says this mother. "He loves watching the kids play and swapping tips with all the parents who are there!"

During times you're distracted by work or holidays, tell your spouse to be ready and available to be with your child. A mother in one of my groups said her two youngsters were impossible at big family gatherings in her house, until she planned some joint approaches with her husband. "It occurred to me," she says, "that the kids might be acting so bratty because they were basically ignored by me for two or three days beforehand while I was getting ready for the holiday." Now whenever there's something busy going on, her husband spends extra time with the children; their behavior has improved.

When one father arrived home from work in the evenings, he really wanted to play with the kids—like many fathers, in a hectic, wrestling way. These two youngsters got so jazzed up they couldn't settle down to sleep, just at the point Mom had had enough of them and wanted them to get to bed. She finally said to her husband: "You want to be with the children and they want to be with you, but they're just getting too wound up having this much action in the evening. Suppose two days a week we let them stay up later to be with you, and on those days I'll see they get a long nap in the afternoon." And then she said to her sons, "Listen, you two, if you want to stay up and play with Dad, you have to have this nap. Then you'll have a good time and still feel okay tomorrow."

You and your mate aren't always going to present a perfect united front to your child. But you should make sure you talk together about behavior problems, and agree on joint approaches. Joint approaches work better because your child isn't confused; he sees that Mom and Dad both mean business, expect the same behavior, and are willing to help him get there. He's not tempted to try to divide and conquer by playing one off against the other.

> **Changes in behavior—yours and your child's—take time. Remember that tomorrow is another day. You'll still be together. And next week is another week.**

So often in my workshops a parent will report on a behavior problem going on with his child, and how he used the tools: He switched "no" to "yes," or he offered choices, or he gave his youngster the words to use. And then he'll say, "But it didn't work." The crying or the dawdling continued for another half an hour, he'll say, or his toddler punched the little kid in preschool again the next day.

But just because the protests or the undesirable actions didn't stop on the spot doesn't mean the tool wasn't working. The child who isn't getting what he wants right then and there is going to be disappointed, maybe furious, and he wants his parent to know that he is. The child who wants to hit or punch is going to have trouble getting control of those impulses.

In fact, when those workshop parents who say the tool was a failure keep talking, it's often clear that something *did* work.

The mother whose little boy always demands one more book read to him before lights-out says she stuck to her guns this time, although he howled; she told him it really was too late and they'd get to that other book tomorrow.

The father who gave his little boy words to use instead of grabbing and hitting says his son told him after preschool, "I only hit two times today."

Maybe the crying or the hitting happened again. But those parents took a step forward; they were getting closer to making real changes. And after two or three or four more similar go-rounds, the chances are excellent that the misbehavior will be gone.

You have to be ready to switch gears too. If one tool is getting you nowhere, try a different approach. In the next chapter, you'll see that correcting a misbehavior is usually a multistep process. Occasionally, absolutely nothing works. Then you might say to your child: "I'm sorry you're unhappy and I'm unhappy. But you know what? I'm sure things will go better tomorrow." Give him hope! Give yourself hope!

There's nothing wrong—there's much to be gained, in fact—in letting your child know that it's hard for you to change too. Say: "I felt terrible when I got so impatient with you this afternoon and started yelling. I'm really going to try hard not to do that anymore." Your youngster gets the idea that you think *you* need to behave better, too, sometimes, and you're working on it. He gets the idea that there's always a second and a third chance, for you and for himself.

Change always takes time. It's a simple but helpful notion to remember that you and your child will still be there tomorrow.

Chapter 4

THE TOOLS IN ACTION, BY AGES AND STAGES:

How to prevent, correct, and encourage . . . and what to do next when what you're doing isn't working.

IN THIS CHAPTER, I'LL SHOW you how the tools work in the most common power struggles that come up between parent and child. I'll often provide sample dialogues, but remember that the exact words aren't important: The idea is to use the tools that work, apply them to your own situations, and say them in your own way and your own words.

For each of these scenarios, I give a brief background to illustrate what's causing your child to act in ways you find difficult. I sometimes tell parents in my workshops to consider themselves Sherlock Holmes or Nancy Drew solving a mystery. When you sleuth out what's *behind* a child's particular behavior, two things happen:

First, you gain a clue that helps you know what to do next. If your child hits another youngster in anger and frustration, or hits out of an excess of joy and excitement, you will in either case stop the hitting, but you may handle it in slightly different ways.

Second, when you know *why* your child is doing something

you don't want her to do—and that almost always she's satisfying a need, and not just trying to get your goat—you feel less annoyed and you're less likely to slip into the nagging mode (which we might define as saying the same thing four times in a row, with ever-increasing volume and vehemence!).

Here's part of the payoff about putting these "solutions" into practice: You don't have to keep on doing so forever. After a while, you don't have to use the tools so often or so lengthily. Everything gets easier.

If your arguments have been about eating, for example, and you follow the routine of offering choices, involving your child in the solution, applying consequences, and so on, and you carry out that scenario three or four times, the food wars decrease; you reach a day when you don't have to go through all that at every meal.

If prying your child away from a play date when it's time to go home has always been a difficult, aggravating business, try the suggestions—setting limits, offering your regrets, letting her get in the last word, and so on—and soon you should be able to gain your child's cooperation with a fraction of that effort.

Your child sees that you're not backing down, you mean business, she does have to go along with the program, but also that you're trying to accommodate and help her. And that changes everything. When democratic discipline really gets cooking, three things happen: You eliminate or at least dramatically reduce the nagging (which makes everybody feel happier); you persuade your child to do what you want or need her to do; and soon, it's infinitely less time-consuming and tiring to get there.

Bear in mind that you may be able to end struggles in one or two areas, but not in others. Maybe the food battles die down, but nothing you try makes much of a dent in the nightly "I won't go to bed!" scene. Give it time. Remember that tomorrow is another day. If you can keep the tools in mind, and reduce the nagging and power struggles in the ways we suggest *65% of the time,* you're doing great.

And enjoy the progress you and your child *have* made.

A mother in one of my workshops was often exhausted from arguing with her strong-willed, high-energy daughter. One of their most difficult daily clashes took place over getting dressed and what the little girl would or wouldn't wear. That mother tried some suggestions we'll outline later in this chapter, and the clothing wars essentially disappeared. Mother and daughter still hit heads in some other areas, but the sense of camaraderie and working together over the dressing issue helped them both.

Mornings were much more pleasant, this mom said. She could start the day not feeling as if she was in for a fight. She saw that her daughter was really capable of change and that *she* could be more effective in helping her child. That's the other payoff: Use the tools, achieve some successes, and you lower the overall level of friction between your child and yourself. You like each other more! Life is more fun!

WHEN YOUR 6-MONTH- TO 1-YEAR-OLD . . .

GRABS DANGEROUS OR FRAGILE OBJECTS.

THE SCENE: Your 10-month-old—practicing her cruising by holding on to and circling the coffee table—makes a sudden lunge for your mug full of tea.

THE BACKGROUND: The baby's world is brand-new, full of strange and wonderful objects that catch her eye. She wants to reach for each thing, take it, explore it—with, of course, no awareness of what's breakable, what's important to you, or what can hurt her.

Eternal vigilance on your part is the first rule of order! Especially once your child starts to move around a bit on her own, you must be ever on the alert against her picking up what is dangerous or fragile.

When it's necessary to keep her from getting at something or to take an object out of her hands, immediately offer her something else. Remove the mug of tea and give her a plastic cup she can hold and bang on the floor.

One "fragile object" your youngster may love to grab is your hair. You're holding your child, and suddenly your head is yanked to one side as she grabs a handful and pulls. Or she may squeeze and push on your nose and cheeks. Take her hands away from your head, put them around your neck, and say:

> **"Ow, that hurts when you squeeze my face. Give me a hug instead. Umm, that feels nice. And I'm giving you a big hug right back."**

If she's fascinated by your eyeglasses, as little children almost always are, and tries to take them off, catch her hand in yours and say:

> **"These are Daddy's glasses. No playing with Daddy's glasses. Let's find something else for you."**

And if you happen to have some plastic sunglasses handy, they're a wonderful substitute.

THE TOOLS: Limit the behavior at once—your child can't be allowed to get at eyeglasses, coffee mugs, pointy pencils, or anything else that could hurt her or break. Offer a substitution and then approve of her new behavior. The good news: At this age, your child will probably be quickly satisfied with the alternate item you've handed her, especially if you encourage her by pointing out what a lot of fun she's having with it and how nicely she's holding it. When she's a little older and more determined to get what she wants, it won't be quite so easy to deflect her attention.

MOUTHS EVERYTHING HE HOLDS.

THE SCENE: Crawling around on the living room rug, your child discovers an old laminated cardboard drinks coaster that got kicked under the table, picks it up, and starts to chew on it.

THE BACKGROUND: Cardboard coasters, house keys, the dog's leash, toys, food—whatever object your child is holding or comes across is likely to go right in his mouth. This is his first line of exploration: hands and then mouth, to see how this thing feels.

Again, parents need to be eternally vigilant. Regularly check the floor and any surfaces your child can reach, to watch out for and remove or anchor down any small objects. Be sure that anything your child handles and plays with is at least one inch by one inch; anything smaller he can swallow.

Also, remember that your small child has a kitten's-eye view of the world. He'll spot objects you don't even know are there, like the bolts underneath a coffee table or the upholstery tacks on the underside of a chair.

While the parents were talking and not paying much attention, a 10-month-old in one of my workshops kept working a loose chair screw with his thumb, freed it, and was about to put it in his mouth. His dad jumped up and said:

> **"Hey! You can't eat that!"**

He grabbed the screw from him and immediately gave him something else to hold and mouth, a big plastic bolt from our toy workbox.

Another youngster liked to sit on the floor next to his mother's chair and chew on her shoes. When she removed the shoes, he started munching on her ankle. He also was determined to grab the cup his mom was holding, and she saw a chance to come up with a good substitution—and, ideally, keep his attention off the shoes and ankles he found so tempting. She handed him two plastic cups, and Michael pretended to pour with them. She told him how well he was holding the cups and pouring, and he was content with this activity for some time.

THE TOOLS: First and foremost, keep your child safe by removing any small, dangerous, or dirty object he's latched onto and is likely to put in his mouth. Offer a safe substitution—if you can, something that looks or feels like the item you've removed. Then remember to approve the new behavior.

SPITS OR THROWS FOOD.

THE SCENE: You've just put a spoonful of strained peas in her mouth; she spits it out. Next, she's flinging banana slices over the side of her high chair tray.

THE BACKGROUND: Don't take it personally. When a child is introduced to solid foods, around 5 or 6 months of age, she finds the texture different from what she's accustomed to—maybe appealing, maybe surprising, maybe not entirely to her liking. One way of exploring or showing disapproval is to spit it out. She also spits if she doesn't feel like eating anymore.

Toward the end of the first year, too, she has the ability to grab things and throw them, and finger foods are likely to go flying.

There's not much to be gained by telling your child she shouldn't spit. Just have her set up in a place where you don't mind a little mess, perhaps with some oilcloth under her chair.

When she throws food, assume that she's finished eating and end the meal. And there's nothing wrong with reminding her:

> **"Food is for eating. Balls are for throwing."**

Give her lots of other opportunities to get in some throwing, with Nerf balls (the firm, multigrip type) or other appropriate items. You might also attach to her high chair, with plastic links, some small toys or balls that can go over the side and get pulled right back up.

THE TOOLS: Substitute, then approve her new behavior: "No, bananas are not to be thrown, but you can throw your ball . . . and look what a lot of fun you're having with that ball!" Give a "yes": "Food is for eating."

MAKES LOUD NOISES OR REPETITIVE SOUNDS.

THE SCENE: You're getting a bite of lunch in your neighborhood restaurant when your 11-month-old, sitting contentedly in his stroller, starts making a loud, shrieky kind of noise. He's having a great time; you and your fellow diners are not.

THE BACKGROUND: During this age, children discover they can make all sorts of interesting sounds, and they enjoy doing so . . . for long stretches at a time.

Stay away from restaurants while your child is in his loud noise phase! When he first discovers his shrieking voice, to his delight, it's pretty hard to get him to turn down the volume. You may be able to catch his attention and quiet him with a whisper or a soft voice of your own, but don't count on it. Allow him to use his loud voice to his heart's content where it won't annoy other people (except maybe you)—in your home, at the beach.

A youngster in my workshop just loved blowing air through his mouth and making his lips vibrate noisily with a "Bbrrrr" sound. He kept this up for a whole hour!
Again, it's a great discovery for a child that he can make this interesting sound, and he wants to repeat it over and over. So, if you can stand it, let him do it for as long as he wants.

THE TOOLS: Say "yes" to the sounds; substitute and redirect by getting him involved with a rattle or some other object when he's making sounds in a restaurant or other place where people will be annoyed.

DEMANDS A NEW ACTIVITY EVERY 10 MINUTES.

THE SCENE: You've set your child up in her crib with her stuffed animals, you've started her off twirling and pushing on her busy box, you think you can grab some time to make a couple of phone calls. Ten minutes is all you get, before she's fussing again for your attention.
THE BACKGROUND: It's a harsh reality, but here it is: During your child's first year, expect that you won't get much of anything done during the day except while she's napping. She *needs,* and demands, a constant change of activities; she'll occupy herself for 10 minutes at a time, after which you'll have to be involved with her again—that's the typical attention span. And if she hasn't been sleeping well at night

and thus is keeping you up, you feel especially irritable at having to be on call twenty-four hours a day.

When your child wants and usually needs a new activity every 10 minutes, here are some ideas on how to cope:

- Strap her in a front or rear baby carrier and talk to her while you're busy around the house. She gets to be involved with you and move from room to room.
- Put her in a playpen stocked with self-activating toys for up to 20 minutes at a time when you need to keep her safe while you're occupied.
- Keep changing toys and playthings. Look for items that allow your child to move and practice skills— kicking with her feet, pulling with her hands, cruising (playpens are great for cruising practice), setting off sounds, pushing buttons.
- Organize your days in a regular pattern with lots of small segments and stick to the routine.

One mother liked to be outside with her child for hours at a time, but the child was always fussy and demanding. Mom set up a new sequence of activities—feeding in the morning, playtime, outdoor trip, nap back home, feeding, bath, play, outdoors again, and so on. After a few days on this routine, her son—who previously was always catching a nap "on the run" outdoors—was noticeably calmer and more settled.

- If you can, devote one low cabinet in your kitchen to child-friendly items—large plastic containers, lids, lightweight pans and pots, plastic measuring cups, measuring spoons (remove the ring, which is small enough to swallow). Every so often, add some new, unfamiliar items. By the time your child is about 10 to 12 months of age (and especially later, when she reaches toddlerhood), she'll like to sit on the kitchen floor, near you, and play with the contents of her

cabinet. While you go about your kitchen chores, talk to her, go over to her regularly and spend a few moments engaged with her in a little joint play.
- Get plenty of outdoor time, which provides refreshing air and lots of stimulating things to see.

Here's your main coping mechanism: Keep your expectations rigorously in line with her abilities. And the reality is, she's not going to be content to lie on her back quietly looking up at the ceiling for very long.

A mother in one of my workshops was feeling quite cranky about her 9-month-old. She said:

> **"I wanted to sit down with my husband and have a peaceful dinner, and Nathan kept demanding attention. I was really annoyed because he'd had my complete attention all day long! He's got to learn that he has to give me my own time in the evening!"**

It's easy to understand her frustration. But 9-month-old Nathan is truly not capable of giving Mom her "own time." The solution? Maybe Nathan's dad can occupy his son while Mom takes a breather. Maybe Mom and Dad will have to sit down to dinner at nine instead of seven o'clock. And *definitely,* Mom has to remember what Nathan can and cannot do at this tender age.

THE TOOLS: Let your child know what to expect by ordering your day's activities in a sequence that becomes predictable to her; some of the fussiness may quiet down and (by around 10 months) she'll be learning to wait and delay gratification more successfully. Get outside time.

Get help! This is a rough year for you. You are, most likely, feeling sleep-deprived, adult-conversation-deprived, positive-feedback-deprived. If you can, hire a baby-sitter some evenings for a couple of hours, and enjoy grown-up time.

Plan joint approaches with your spouse. Figure out together how and when your spouse will relieve you of baby-tending duties or if it would be helpful to make changes in breakfast or dinner schedules.

GETS CLINGY.

THE SCENE: Your 7-month-old won't let you out of his sight, won't let you put him down, won't let anyone else come near, much less pick him up.

THE BACKGROUND: Those are the typical behaviors that go with separation anxiety, which usually hits babies between 6 months (in some precocious children, as early as 4 months) and 1 year of age.

Most parents can accept and handle it calmly in an infant, but become concerned if their 1½- or 2-year-old begins acting fussy in those ways. They start thinking, "Uh-oh, he's turning into a clingy kid, we've got to get baby-sitters and go out more so he gets used to not having me around all the time."

They shouldn't worry. A child who's gone through the first year without noticeable separation anxiety will get it later, usually around 17 to 22 months. Or maybe he's just having another round for good measure.

During a clingy stage:

Don't make big changes—in baby-sitters, routine, and so on. Keep life consistent. Unless absolutely necessary, keep trips away from home to one or two days.

Be prepared for a sudden switch to clingy behavior. One baby had enjoyed a friendly visit from his grandparents, who carried and played with him for a long time. When Grandma and Grandpa came for another visit two weeks later, the youngster screamed and fussed when he saw them. The grandparents understood that the child was in a separation/stranger anxiety stage, and waited until later in the day when he felt ready to accept them.

Let him know each time you're leaving, even if you'll be gone for only a few minutes. If he clings and fusses when you go in the bathroom, leave the door open (if you don't mind) so that he can see you and be reassured.

Don't make him wait too long for his meals. Fill up his needs before they're desperate and give him a little more of yourself after feeding—play with him, read to him, sing to him a bit. Let him sit on your lap while you're on the phone.

In short, don't push him away; if you do, he's likely to become even more clingy and perhaps genuinely frightened. Wait out the clingy stage. It'll be over in a couple of months.

THE TOOLS: Help your child through a clingy stage by letting him know what comes next.

WHEN YOUR 1-YEAR- TO 18-MONTH-OLD . . .

HATES THE STROLLER.

THE SCENE: You've just left the house with your 1½-year-old, you pick her up and put her in the stroller, and she hits the roof. She's screaming, arching her back, shouting "Out! Out!" Or: You've made it comfortably to the store, but once inside, she's determined to be let loose from that stroller.

THE BACKGROUND: When she sees the two of you are getting ready to go outside, she thinks, "Hooray! I'm going to run around and have a good time." Then she gets strapped in a contraption that won't let her move. She can't yet understand there must be a delay in getting from here to there. She wants *out*!

And there's another reason for the protests, one that applies to stroller-hating and other behavioral issues that surface at this age. When a child reaches age 1, she starts telling you, "I'm here, and I want to direct the show!" She tells you that not with words, but by fighting the stroller, grabbing everything in sight, touching all new and fascinating objects, and scampering away from you at every opportunity.

You think, "This child just doesn't listen, she doesn't seem to hear." Many parents are in your boat.

Attach stroller toys across the stroller and change them often; having something to play with and work on can make her more content to stay put.

If your child is refusing to get in the stroller and arching her back when you attempt to seat her, there's not always a lot you can do to correct the situation. You may need either to strap her in, howling, and get moving, or to give in to the ruckus and let her walk (but she must hold your hand).

If your child is refusing to stay in the stroller while you're shopping, say:

> "I know how much you hate being in that stroller while we're in the store. We have to buy some socks here today, so let's go find the socks and you can hold them while we finish."

Suppose she calms down until you're almost done, then can't stand waiting at the cashier's register one more second.

Appeal to the cashier. Tell the cashier you have about 2 more minutes to get out of the store, because your child's attention span isn't going to last longer than that. Ask if there's a piece of receipt tape or some other goody behind the counter that your child can hold and play with for those 2 minutes. Sometimes, you have to just get out of there. Tell the cashier you can't finish the transaction right now, you're going outside for a while and you'll come back later.

THE TOOLS: Empathize. Even a child this young will understand from the tone of your voice that you know she's unhappy and you wish it were otherwise. Offer substitutions; your child may be pleasantly distracted by a pair of socks and also may feel more a part of the goings-on.

Be on your child's side; she does want to cooperate, she just doesn't know how. It's embarrassing to be the grown-up in this scene your child is creating, but you don't owe apologies to the cashier or anyone else.

.   .   .

Many parents in my workshops say they can't go out on errands with their 1- or 1½-year-olds and get anything much accomplished at all. Prevention may be the best solution. It's not always possible to leave a child home with the other parent or a sitter, but if it is, do so. Tell your child:

> **"I know you like going to the store with me, but it's just too hard for you to stay in the stroller right now, and you do have to be in the stroller so I can keep track of you while we're shopping. So for now, you're going to stay home with Daddy (or Mommy) when I go to the store."**

THE TOOLS: Be empathetic. Let her know the consequence of her behavior is that she can't go with you right now, but someday she will—that's giving her hope.

WANTS TO TOUCH OR GRAB ALL NEW OR FASCINATING OBJECTS.

THE SCENE: At play group, your child sees another youngster holding a toy radio, walks over, and takes it out of his hand. At home, your child scoots right past his box full of toys, determined to get at the Dustbuster in the corner of the living room or at the VCR to push those buttons.

THE BACKGROUND: The 14- or 16- or 18-month-old is so full of curiosity, he wants to touch and explore anything new and different. And when another child is playing with something, he finds that object *especially* fascinating; he feels he ought to have it, even if he's happy with what he's got.

One mother worried that her daughter was turning out to be a bully: 14-month-old Lilly was always grabbing toys from other children. Lilly was in no way a bully, and not yet old enough to know about taking turns, but she *did* need to begin to learn not to yank things away from other people.

Lilly's mother tried to anticipate her child's interest and set her up with some appealing objects as soon as they arrived at the play group. When Lilly went after another child's toy, Mom quickly intervened:

> **"Lilly, Andrea is playing with that radio right now. When she's finished with it you can use it. Let's look at what else you can have."**

She'd then find a similar toy, one that also had knobs to twirl, and get her youngster started with it.

On the home front, even though you've removed, covered up, or anchored down everything that could be dangerous for your child to get his hands on, he'll still find an object you don't want him to have . . . and head for it over and over.

Remember the tool: limit, substitute, approve. When he's determined to get at that Dustbuster, first limit his behavior by stashing the object away, out of sight. Buy a plastic cover (available in baby supply stores or through catalogs) that fits over your VCR control panel. Second, offer a safe and reasonable substitution: He's probably not going to be put off by your handing him one of his old, familiar toys, but might be delighted by the chance to push your (unplugged) vacuum cleaner around the floor. Then, get down on the floor with him, help him get started, and approve the new behavior:

> "You know, you're getting to be a strong little guy! You can push that old vacuum cleaner around wherever you want it to go."

THE TOOLS: Offering a substitution is the primary tool, but don't expect your child to accept it gratefully. Help him invest his attention and energy in something else by approving of what he's doing with that new object. Expect to put in some time and effort on it all.

When you stop your child from grabbing someone else's toy and lead him toward another plaything, tell him what to expect and give him hope. Say he'll have a chance later at the coveted object. Even if "later" doesn't mean much to him right now, you're sowing small seeds about sharing and taking turns.

RUNS AWAY IN OPEN SPACES.

THE SCENE: You've just reached the playground with your 15-month-old and unstrapped her from the stroller. Suddenly she takes off, not looking back and paying no attention to your calls to stop.

THE BACKGROUND: From the time your child starts to feel pretty steady on two feet until around age 3, running away is going to be a problem, and it's one we'll talk about here and in the next two age categories. At this very young age, she absolutely cannot be counted on to stay next to you or to stop at your command. You must run after her at once or hold on to prevent a sudden bolt.

Although she's still too young to grasp the whole idea, tell her what's going on and what will happen someday. Say:

> "I have to keep you safe and that means I have to hold on to you right now. When you're able to walk next to me without me worrying that you'll run off, I'll let you do that."

Many parents frown on the idea of using a harness with a young child. If you can overcome your feelings that it's too much like walking a dog on a leash, securing your youngster in this way might be useful and sensible at times. A simple wrist tether allows your child to walk about five feet away from you, and have both hands free to pick up leaves or touch the display windows or fire hydrants you're passing. It's a good way to get safely from here to there without her being confined to a stroller or required to clasp your hand. I recently saw young children wrist-tethered in this way, and both were happily walking along, seemingly oblivious of their parents' presence. Your child feels more independent, and you're reassured that if she starts to go flying off, you've got a firm hold on her.

THE TOOLS: When it comes to safety, there can be no negotiation or compromise; don't give your child the benefit of the doubt that she'll be able to stay next to you. This is an <u>insist</u>! But you can always give a little hope—let her know that someday she'll be big enough to walk without you holding on.

TRIES TO CLIMB WHENEVER POSSIBLE.

THE SCENE: While you're in the bathroom brushing your teeth, your 13-month-old comes in and climbs up on the toilet seat. You grab her just in time to prevent a nosedive.

THE BACKGROUND: Even before your youngster can run, jump, or even walk very well, she'll start to climb. She *needs* to practice climbing, and she'll take every chance to do so . . . although she may not know how to get back down.

Keep areas off-limits as necessary. If she's always tempted to climb up on your bed, keep the bedroom door closed while you're not in that room. If she follows you into the bathroom and starts climbing up the toilet or bathtub, remove her and give her a short explanation of what you have to do. Say:

> "Honey, I'm going to be in the bathroom for a little while. I know you like coming in with me, but it's too hard for you to resist climbing up on the toilet, and I don't want you to do that. You can stay and play on the floor right outside and you can watch me."

Then, find other ways for her to practice climbing. A stable step stool at home is good. Take her to the playground every day, and supervise her very carefully as she goes up and down the first few steps on the play gym. Hold her hand as you walk along the street and stop so she can climb a building's steps. You *can't stop* her from climbing and you don't want to; you *can* give lots of chances to do so safely.

THE TOOLS: Instead of "No, don't go up there, you'll get hurt," give your child a "yes"—"Yes, you can climb, and here's where you will do it." Offer substitutions; high beds and toilet seats and a flight of stairs aren't part of the deal, but a sturdy step stool and the steps on the playground slide (holding on to your hand) can take their place. Get lots of outdoor time while your youngster is in a major climbing stage.

BITES, HITS, OR PUSHES.

THE SCENE: As you're snuggling with your 17-month-old, he tries to take a bite out of your shoulder. It hurts! At a family gathering, he knocks his little cousin over to get at the dollhouse he wants to play with.

THE BACKGROUND: Biting, hitting, and pushing are some of the child's first real efforts to assert himself. Maybe he's feeling excited, angry, affectionate, or in an exploring mood. Maybe he wants to make contact. Maybe he just wants to get from here to there and another child is in his path.

Eventually, he learns there's a better, gentler way to get your attention or something else he wants. But biting, hitting, and pushing (aggressive behaviors, though not always aggressively intended) are going to go on for several years. Here and in the next two age categories we talk about different ways children display those behaviors.

When you're holding your youngster against your shoulder and he seems to want to take a nip out of it, he may be teething . . . or he may be showing you that he loves you and thinks you taste good. That kind of bite comes in place of a kiss, but you still want to help him learn the better way. If it hurts, say so:

> **"Ouch! We have to be soft."**

Gently pull his face away from your shoulder, give him a kiss, run your fingers over his lips and cheek, and say:

> **"Ooh, see how nice and smooth with the fingers. Smooth on your cheek, smooth on your lips."**

A 1½-year-old in my workshop pushed another child over and out of his way, determined to get to the sorting box. His father says Jack is doing a lot of hitting and pushing these days in his constant efforts to explore; Dad, appropriately, keeps an eagle eye out and stays ready to intervene. This day, he picked his son up and said:

> **"Jack, pushing is no good. Let's go over here for a while and we'll play with something else."**

Jack went along with his father, struggling and wiggling for a bit. A few minutes later he found a way to scoot around and get at the sorting box from the other side, and nobody was knocked down.

THE TOOLS: Even when you know your child isn't biting, pushing, or hitting out of anger, stop it (this is another <u>insist</u>). He has to learn that he can't barrel over other people or hurt them. Let him know the impact of what he's doing—"That hurts!" Substitute a gentler behavior and demonstrate how it works, or redirect his attention away from the object he's pushing to get at.

WHEN YOUR 18-MONTH- TO 2-YEAR-OLD . . .

HITS OR PUSHES.

THE SCENE: A bunch of toddlers are gathered for the weekly play group in one child's home. All goes smoothly for about 15 minutes. Then, for no apparent reason, your child hits another youngster, who bursts into tears.

THE BACKGROUND: A young child hits or shoves for any one of several reasons: He wants something another child has, or doesn't want to give up what he has; he's happy and overly excited; he's frustrated and doesn't know what he wants; he needs attention; he wants to be affectionate. As he gains more language and control (and learns that hugs are the best way to be affectionate), hitting subsides.

In the play group, watch your child to find out what's prompting the hitting. Parents tend to overestimate the social skills of a child this age. A group of five or six youngsters may be too much for your child to handle, and he'll do better in a group of three or four.

If he hits or shoves when another child gets too close, help him learn a better way. Later, tell him:

> "Here's what you can do next time if somebody comes too close to you. Put your hands out in front of you and say, 'Stay away.' That's how you can tell him you don't want him coming right next to you."

One 2½-year-old loved the kitchen set in preschool, and as soon as another child reached for the frying pan or the little tin kettle, he punched her away. His mother gave him words to use:

> "I know it's very difficult for you right now to let the other kids use the kitchen. If somebody wants to use the frying pan and you're playing with it, tell her, 'Ask me for the frying pan. Don't grab it.' "

She tried to stay nearby during play dates and for part of the preschool morning while her son was in this pushing and hitting stage. She reminded him as they walked to school in the morning:

> "Remember that when you play with the kitchen it's going to be hard for you when other kids want to play too. When I'm still in the room, you can ask me to help you. If José wants to play with the kitchen like he did yesterday, you and I can find something else for you to do, okay? And then maybe tomorrow we can go a few minutes earlier so you can play with those things before everybody else comes."

A toddler was sitting on his mother's lap while his newborn sibling was resting in Dad's arms nearby. He watched his father playing with the baby, then suddenly gave his mom a hard swat.

The toddler might have needed to let off a little frustration and jealousy, and didn't know exactly what he wanted or how to ask for it. He might just as easily have jumped off Mom's lap and gone over to give the *baby* a swat! Sometimes, too, a youngster gets boisterous and hits his parent out of excitement.

If he hits his baby brother or sister, don't yell at him. Instead, say:

> **"The rule in this family is no hitting. Let's make the baby laugh and not cry."**

And then demonstrate how to make funny faces and sounds or play a peekaboo game that gets baby gurgling.

If he hits you, repeat the family rule about no hitting; then say:

> **"You know, when someone hits me I really don't want to play with that person for a while. Remember when you were playing with Timmy and he hit you and you didn't like it? Well, I don't like it either. Let's have you calm down and then we can start fresh and play again."**

THE TOOLS: Use empathy: "It's going to be hard for you when other kids want to use the kitchen." Insist on certain behavior: "No hitting." To help your child master his urge to hit and shove, give him a substitution—"Put your hands up," or "Let's make the baby laugh"—and words to use—"Stay away," or "Ask me if you want to use the frying pan." Tell him the impact of his behavior and give him a consequence: If he hits you, it makes you unhappy and in no mood to be particularly nice to him for a while. And as much as you can, be a play date supervisor to give him reminders and encouragement as he's learning not to hit.

SHAKES LOOSE OF YOUR HAND OUTDOORS AND RUNS OFF.

THE SCENE: As soon as you get outside, your 1½-year-old pulls her hand out of yours and heads off down the street.
THE BACKGROUND: This is going to be happening for the next several years. As soon as she starts feeling a little independent, a child relishes the heady sense of freedom that comes from letting go of Mom or Dad and taking off.

If her shaking loose and running away from you is a persistent and worrisome problem, tell her she'll have to ride in the stroller for a while until you can be sure she'll keep holding hands. If she generally has enough control to calm down and cooperate, you can help her understand that holding hands is necessary for at least part of the time you're outdoors. Say:

> "You have to hold my hand when we leave home and as we're walking to the park. Once we cross all the streets and we're right outside the park, you can run on your own. If you want to run right now, we can run down the street together."

And then, you can help her look into the future a little further and see a long-term goal. Say:

> "When you get a little older, you'll be able to walk down the block on your own. I want you to be able to do that, but first I have to know that you'll be able to stop at a certain point, and soon we can practice that."

While your child is still a toddler, "when you're older" and "soon" don't have much meaning, but your promising tone may be helpful in encouraging her to stay with the program. Little by little, you can work on the promise. Practice on a side street. Tell her she can walk on her own as far as the tree halfway down the block or the doorway of the next building. And say:

> "If it gets too exciting for you and you just can't stop, I'm going to catch up with you and then we'll hold hands again the rest of the way."

THE TOOLS: You'll be conducting these "going on your own" lessons all through your child's early years. Give her hope right from the start that what she can't do today, she will be able to do eventually, and you'll show her how. Set clear limits and consequences: "It's my job to keep you safe, and if you run off we'll have to take the stroller next time or we'll have to wait a little longer before we practice 'no hands.'" Give her a "yes": "If you want to run more, we can run together down the street."

GETS UPSET WHEN HE CAN'T PRACTICE NEW THINGS.

THE SCENE: Your 19-month-old is intrigued by the snap-it straps on his high chair and stroller, and is determined to get them open. When you pull his hands away from the strap, he flies into a rage.

THE BACKGROUND: At this age, your youngster wants to turn things on and off, twist knobs, pull things, take things apart and push them together again. He's both having some fun and practicing new skills.

His main aim isn't to get out of the chair or stroller, but obviously, to keep your child secured you need to deflect his attention from the safety straps. Find similar objects—a fanny pack, for example, which has a snap-it strap, or plastic, pop-it type links—and keep them nearby for him to work on.

One little boy just loved turning lights on and off, and would drag a chair over to the kitchen switch and flick it on and off, on and off. His dad said:

> "You can't turn the light off and on when I'm cooking. I might get hurt. But suppose you turn this flashlight on and off instead."

A 1½-year-old in one of my parent-child workshops loved to pull people's hair and clothing. His mom realized Bradley wasn't angry or feeling mean . . . he just liked to pull! So at the beginning of play group, she tried to set him up with pull toys, like corn poppers and wagons. At home, she let him pull the vacuum cleaner around by the hose. She also got Brad a doll with lots of hair, and showed him how to pat and stroke it, giving him a little praise along the way:

> "You're doing that so nicely, Brad. It's nice to be gentle and pat the dolly's hair."

THE TOOLS: To cut down on undesirable turning, twisting, pulling, and so on, figure out what your child is "working on" at the moment and come up with suitable substitutions. Keep your eyes open for run-of-the-mill ways he can do that practicing. Maybe he can turn the cold water faucet on and off while you're washing his hands, or help you turn the knobs on the dishwasher. Give approval: "You're doing that so nicely."

WON'T LET OTHER CHILDREN PLAY WITH HER THINGS.

THE SCENE: Your youngster always looks forward to having one of her friends come over for a play date, but as soon as the friend picks up one of her toys, she grabs it back. It's not necessarily her favorite, most special toy—she doesn't want her friend to touch *any* of her stuff.

THE BACKGROUND: Letting someone else use her things is so hard for a young child. That intensely possessive stage may start around age 1½ and go on for a couple of years . . . and almost every parent can't stand it. We hate to see our normally sweet child seemingly acting "selfish"; we tell her she must learn to *share*.

It helps to know that kids have to go through this I-my-mine stage; they need to develop a sense of possession before they can relinquish it. In the meantime, you can pave the way for lessons in sharing and help playtimes run more smoothly.

Before the next play date, say to your child:

> "You know what always happens here, Lexie? You like it when Renee comes over, but when she gets here it's hard for you to let her use your things and she gets upset. So today, let's decide in advance which toys she can play with and

> which aren't okay. The ones you don't want her to use we'll put up in the closet for the time being.
>
> "And here's another thing we can do. I'll ask Renee's mother to bring some of Renee's toys over, so you can both be playing with some of her things too."

Let her pick out the items that she wants off-limits, and ask her again if it's going to be all right for Renee to play with the remaining toys.

Stay nearby or in the same room—these children are too young to play alone. Keep an ear open to monitor the goings-on and be ready to redirect their play at regular, probably 10-minute intervals. If she's able to share, give your child a compliment later on:

> "Renee looked like she was having a lot of fun today. It made a big difference when you decided what toys she could use. I was really happy you could do that."

If matters don't seem to be improving, suspend the indoor play dates for a while. Let your child know why:

> "It's too tough for you right now to invite Renee over here. For the next few times, we'll meet in the park and you two can have a play date outdoors."

THE TOOLS: Get her involved in the solutions to the difficulties she's having. Be a play date supervisor, since you know she'll have difficulty following through on the decisions you've made. Give her some praise for nice behavior; tell her it made everyone feel good. Impose consequences if play doesn't go well, but be empathetic: "I know it's hard sharing your things, so right now we won't invite Renee here but you can play together in the park."

REPEATS ACTIVITIES HE'S BEEN TOLD NOT TO DO.

THE SCENE: Every time you and your 2-year-old sit down to have lunch, he wants to eat your food—off your plate—and drink your iced tea—out of your mug. You tell him to cut it out . . . again and again.

THE BACKGROUND: Your child, with his great desire to explore and test, wants to give everything a try. And when you say "no," something becomes even more enticing.

The father whose toddler kept taking over his lunch was getting very resentful of his son—he felt he couldn't even have his favorite diet iced tea anymore! One day, instead of his usual "no, no, no," he tried a different tack. He said:

> "Freddy, let's talk about what belongs to me and what belongs to you. This is my drink and my plate, and that's your drink and your plate. Now I know you like to taste my drink because you like to taste everything Daddy has. But this is my mug and my tea, and that's your mug and your milk. If you want some juice or some water instead, I'll be glad to give you that. Would you like juice or water instead?"

Freddy, a little surprised by this line of talk, said no. Dad handed him his cup, picked up his own cup, and as they had their drinks, Dad gave him some approval:

> "Look at how well you hold your mug. You can drink right along with me. Isn't it nice that we can both have our drinks and our lunch together?"

For the next several lunchtimes, the father repeated a version of this routine; eventually, Freddy stopped reaching for Dad's meal.

Vanessa's mother was trying to get her 18-month-old to stop picking up her father's business papers. Although Vanessa was told repeatedly she was to stay away from Dad's desk, the little girl was determined to explore those appealing papers. Finally, Mom armed herself with a substitution. When Vanessa headed for the desk, her mother handed her one of her own books and a magazine. They sat on the floor together for a few minutes and looked through the books and magazines together, and then Mom said:

> "You're really good at turning pages now, you know that? This is kind of fun, isn't it, looking through these magazines together."

THE TOOLS: Remember the tool: limit, substitute, and—especially—approve. Approving the new behavior is what will make this correction "take": If your child feels the new item and the new activity are really rather neat and he's doing really rather well with them, he doesn't feel so deprived and ornery because he can't have or do what he's been after. Offer choices when you can. Label what is his—that's giving him a "yes."

HAS A TEMPER TANTRUM.

THE SCENE: You walk into the bathroom and find your toddler squeezing toothpaste into her mouth and eating it. When you remind her that toothpaste isn't for eating and take the tube away, she starts screaming and slamming her hands on the sink.

THE BACKGROUND: Sometime around the middle of her second year, your child is likely to get going full blast with temper tantrums. Almost anything will start her off, and although not all tantrums include kicking and screaming, there's no doubt that your youngster is in high dudgeon!

It helps to remember that to some extent a tantrum may relate to exploring relationships and developing autonomy. With a limited vocabulary and limited skills, your toddler has a hard time expressing feelings when she's unable to do or get something. Also, she can't think ahead very far. She doesn't know about "later" or "soon" or "tomorrow," so she has trouble giving in or waiting, even for a few moments.

The mother of the toothpaste-eating daughter said:

> "I know you're angry right now, just like Oscar on Sesame Street. But toothpaste is no good to eat."

More screaming and protesting from the girl. Mom persevered:

> "Here's what you can do with toothpaste. You can squeeze it out of the tube onto your brush. And you can brush your teeth with it two times a day. And you know what? There are some mints that taste just like this that are okay for you to eat, and maybe we can get some of those."

Mom demonstrated how she could squeeze the toothpaste out of the tube onto the brush, and although she was still teary she became interested, despite herself, in squeezing that toothpaste. She also let her put toothpaste on Mom's brush when she needed it. After a few days, she became competent at applying just the right amount of toothpaste to the brush, and felt pretty good about that. Her mother let her have some Junior Mints, which she enjoyed as well.

THE TOOLS: Your child's temper tantrums are likely to be part of your life for some time to come. Empathize, offer a substitution, and spend some time trying to get her engaged with it. Insist that the screaming behavior does have to stop— and then be prepared to wait it out. In the next age category, you'll find some other ideas on how to handle temper tantrums.

THROWS THINGS.

THE SCENE: Your 1½-year-old thinks it's great fun to toss his bottle of juice or milk into the toilet bowl.
THE BACKGROUND: A child this age has a great desire to throw, whether it's a bottle into the toilet, food off the high chair, toys out of the stroller. He likes to see and hear things drop, or disappear and then reappear. And of course it's lots of fun to involve Mom or Dad in a little game of retrieving the tossed object.

The mother whose youngster kept throwing his bottle in the toilet realized that part of the attraction was the sound of splashing water. She gave him a better place to do his bottle-throwing and water play. She said:

> "You really like to throw your bottle, don't you?
> I'm going to give you a good place to do it. I'll
> help you pull a chair over to the kitchen sink,
> and we can fill it up with some water and you
> can throw it into the sink."

Sometimes she put a pan with water on the kitchen floor, and let her child plop things in the water and pour with small plastic cups while she fixed dinner nearby. The child continued for a while to find the bottle in the toilet a tempting idea, and Mom had to remove him firmly saying, "No, this isn't the place to throw a bottle." (At that, he'd smile—getting in the last word and saying in effect, "I'm competent and you haven't stopped me completely!")

You might need to give your child something *else* to throw. A little boy in one of my workshops was flinging his plastic container of Cheerios at other children. His mom said:

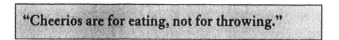

> "Cheerios are for eating, not for throwing."

She led him over to a basket of foam balls and together they played throwing games for a while.

The point is, your child *needs* to practice throwing, and you can shift that need to appropriate objects and places. Let him throw your empty plastic bottles in the recycling bin or papers in the trash basket, for example, and then tell him he did that very well. (And if toys going over the side of the stroller or food over the high chair is a problem, attach some objects with links so your youngster can toss them over and then pull them back up.)

THE TOOLS: Instead of a "no," give a "yes"—"You <u>can</u> throw things, and I'm going to show you what and where." Give your child a substitution—"The toilet is off-limits but the sink is okay; Cheerios are a no-no but foam balls are fun."

———————

WHEN YOUR 2- TO 3-YEAR-OLD . . .

BITES, HITS, OR PUSHES.

THE SCENE: The preschool teacher expresses some concern that your child is aggressive and rough with his classmates. This afternoon, he bit somebody.

THE BACKGROUND: By now, your child is probably away several hours a day in preschool, and dealing with the frustrations that come from holding his place in a group of youngsters. By now, too, he might have a baby brother or sister in his life, an addition he finds a mixed blessing.

All those aggressive feelings sometimes get the better of him and disintegrate into physical acting out; some kids at age 4 are still pushing and pinching when things aren't going right. Again, find the meaning behind the behavior; you'll stop it in any case, but your responses will be different depending on what's going on.

A 3-year-old girl was aiming a lot of pushes and punches at her mother, who was several months pregnant. It wasn't hard for Mom to figure out that Maryann was worried about this new baby soon to be in her scene. After one especially "acting out" afternoon, Maryann's mother talked to her the next day:

> **"You know, honey, you've been pushing and hitting me a lot lately, and I think maybe you're trying to hurt the baby. You need to know that after the baby is born, I'll still love you, we'll still read together, we'll still go to the park together, we'll still go in the wading pool. A lot of things are going to change but that isn't going to change, because you'll always be my special girl."**

The mother of 3-year-old Ellen was nursing her 2-month-old one afternoon. She interrupted nursing and left the room to answer a phone call, and while on the phone heard the baby let out a yelp. When she asked Ellen what had happened, the little girl feigned ignorance. Mom persevered and told Ellen it was important she know why the baby was screaming. Ellen said, "By accident I bit his foot. My teeth just slipped." They talked some more:

> Mom: **"Hmmm . . . your teeth slipped. Let's figure out why your teeth slipped. Was it because they got loose? Was it because the sun was out?** [Ellen is grinning a little sheepishly.] **Was it because the baby was crying and you felt mad at him?"**
> Ellen said yes.
> Mom: **"You know, this happened to me sometimes when I was younger. I felt like biting my brother. But my mom was there to help me and I'm here to help you too, because I can't let you bite Kevin. I can't let him get hurt, just like I can't let you get hurt. So, what do you think you can do the next time you feel like biting him?"**

> Ellen: "Maybe I'll go somewhere else and he'll be in another room and I won't see him."
> Mom: "Good idea. Okay, that's a deal."

One 3-year-old was doing a lot of shoving and some biting in nursery school when other kids interfered with his play or took something away from him. His father talked to him about how important it was to use words when he felt angry—"I'm playing with this now, you can't have it now." Dad also gave him some actions to take to "buy himself some time." He said:

> "Richard, I want you to try something in school. The next time you want to hit or bite somebody, put your hands behind your back and take three big breaths. While you're doing that, you'll be able to think of what you can say to that kid to let him know that you're mad."

This little trick worked like a charm. A few days later Richard told his parents that he didn't hit anybody all week, and it was clear he took real pride in being able to manage himself.

THE TOOLS: Sometimes it's wise to first let emotions die down; wait until later to make corrections, because your child has trouble hearing you when he's feeling aggressive and it takes time for him to process what you're saying.

And if you can, lighten up the mood. Like many parents, you probably get most upset at what seems like rough, mean behavior on your child's part; you envision your 3-year-old growing up to be a thug. If you can use a little humor while you set limits and help him find the gentler way, everybody feels better and he knows you're on his side.

Let him know the impact of his behavior—when you kick me, it hurts; when you push somebody, they don't like you so much. Give him words to use and substitute actions to take. And then, by the time he's getting to be 3 and older, he should be expected to make up for misbehavior. If he pushes, he may apologize or, more important, make amends.

WHINES.

THE SCENE: "I want juice . . . I want juice . . . juice, juice . . . pleeeeze!" Your toddler is letting you know she wants juice right now, and it's not what she says but the way she says it—that high-pitched, singsongy, pitiful-sounding wail—that is driving you crazy.

THE BACKGROUND: Whining usually starts around age 2½, when a child would like to cry, feels she's too old to cry, but desperately wants to get through to Mom or Dad. I tell parents in my workshops to think of it as cry-talk.

The whining instinct can persist until she's 4 or 5 or older. Usually, a very young child whines because she wants something, can't yet verbalize well, and has a hard time delaying gratification for even 5 more minutes. Youngsters also whine when they're cranky and tired, when they want things they know they can't have, when they feel life—i.e., Mom and/or Dad—is being unfair.

Then there's whining in the form of nagging (especially from 3- and 4-year-olds), which develops when a child has learned that keeping up the whining and begging eventually works to get her what she wants: She asks for a snack on the checkout line or a toy in the mall, the parent says "no" three times in a row, and then, finally worn down, buckles and gives in to the snack or toy. A pattern is set, one that's hard to break.

When your child begins one of these high, fine whines, leave the room for a minute and take some deep breaths. Then go back to your child, get down to her level, and say:

> **"I would really like to hear what you have to say, but you have to use a voice I can listen to. Okay, that's better, that's a voice I can hear. Now tell me what you want to say."**

And then, of course, be prepared to listen.

Another idea:

> **"Oh, that whiny voice you're using hurts my ears so much. Ouch, do my ears hurt! What can we do to stop this? Let's erase the blackboard and start over."**

If you and your youngster have a generally cooperative relationship, she may be willing and able to cut the whining right off and speak in her normal voice—it really is delightful to watch a child simply change course. (When one mother said this to her 3-year-old, her daughter did stop but also reminded her mom, "Don't say 'whining,' Mommy, it's 'cry-talk.'")

Sometimes you need to recognize that your child is whiny because she's been expected to play on her own for too long or feels excluded. Give her some more of you.

A 3-year-old was making dinnertime unpleasant for her parents with whining, until her father stopped the grown-up conversation and said:

> **"You know what, Kate? I think you don't
> understand what Mommy and Daddy were
> talking about. You want to join in our talk too."**

Mom and Dad started including Kate and the whining
stopped.

When you have been repeatedly buckling in the face of
your child's nagging and whining, breaking the pattern is
going to take time.

First, instead of immediately locking yourself in with a
"no" to your child's initial request—and starting her off on
the whining that leads you to give in—tell her you need a
minute to think about it. Then evaluate if your "no" is
reasonable: A snack on the checkout line might make sense, if
you've already been there a long time and the line is long;
picking up a small toy at the mall might make sense, if your
youngster hasn't had a special treat in a while.

Second, stop yourself from making meaningless threats, in
general. If you've imposed for some behavior the consequence
of no TV for the next month, both you and your child will
find it too hard to keep to. She'll start nagging and whining
and you'll reverse your position. The pattern is reinforced.

Third, when you do issue a firm "no" and you've set a
sensible consequence—no play dates for the next two days—
hold firm.

If you've been having a major whining issue in your
household, been working with your child on cutting out the cry-
talk, and then gone through a pleasant day or weekend when she
really did cut it out, give her some applause. Say:

> **"You've been asking for things in such a nice
> way. I haven't heard the cry-talk all weekend.
> It's so much more pleasant for us to be together."**

THE TOOLS: Know your trigger points and give yourself a time-out so you won't respond angrily; simmer down before you try to correct your child's behavior. Use a little humor or exaggeration—the sight of you clapping your hands over your ears in imaginary pain will make your child smile.

Hesitate before you say "no," and see if a "yes" would be reasonable under the circumstances. When a "no" is important, stick to it.

When you're getting nowhere, announce you're erasing the blackboard and starting over.

If the behavior changes, let her know you've noticed and tell her how good you feel because of it.

SAYS "NO" TO EVERYTHING, EVEN TO ACTIVITIES OR FOODS SHE LIKES.

THE SCENE: You tell your child to brush her teeth; she says "No." You ask her if she'd like orange or apple juice; she picks orange, but when you hand it to her, she says "No, don't want it."

THE BACKGROUND: Two to three is the age of "no." All kids go through this stage, some to a more aggravating (to parents) degree than others. Saying "no" is your child's asserting herself. It's a way of declaring, "I'm me. I have my identity and you have yours. I'm Douglas [or Emily]. Now that I've made that clear, maybe I can go along with what you want."

When your youngster gets a little older and a little more competent, when she has a good grasp on the language and physical skills that help her get through her day with more ease and less frustration, the "no's" will die down. It will take all your patience not to nag, but if you can help her through this negative stage with respect, you'll be rewarded.

Make life easier on yourself and reduce the power struggles by letting your child get away with a "no" when it doesn't really matter. When it *does* matter and you *can't* agree to her "no," hold firm and explain what you're up to. The mother whose daughter wanted no part of toothbrushing said:

> "I know you don't like brushing your teeth. But my job as your mom is to protect your teeth and make sure they stay clean and healthy. So the deal is, if you want to be able to eat some of your favorite things, like chips and cookies, you'll have to have your teeth brushed. I really do want you to know how to do this by yourself, and I'm going to keep showing you how. But for now, I'll have to do it."

After a few days of holding firm, she found that when her child wanted to get some cookies or treats, the little girl came over and said, "Have you brushed my teeth? Will you brush my teeth now?"

You ask your child if she'd like chocolate or strawberry ice cream, and she picks chocolate. You hand her the dish of chocolate ice cream, and she says, "No. Don't want it." You might say:

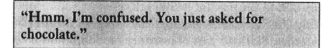

> "Hmm, I'm confused. You just asked for chocolate."

You start to put the ice cream away, and she says, "Want it."
This is typical "no" behavior. Don't put the food right away and if she changes her mind, don't say, "No, now I'm

not going to give it to you." Let her have it. Remember that she's just asserting herself, not trying to give you grief.

THE TOOLS: Negotiate and offer choices when that makes sense. When there's no room for compromise, empathize and offer your regrets that she has to do the thing she's saying "no" to. Give her hope that soon she'll be more in control.

WON'T LET GO OF AN OBJECT OR ACTIVITY HE SEEMED TO BE FINISHED WITH.

THE SCENE: You and your toddler have had a lovely hour at the natural history museum, enjoying the displays and trying out all the interactive exhibits. As you're making your way to the exit, your child sees another kid looking at the dinosaur diorama, pushes him away, and says, "You can't look at the dinosaur." A little farther down the hall, your child punches the buttons on the interactive game he's already played, just so another little boy who's approaching can't use it.
THE BACKGROUND: It's not only toys that your 2- or 3-year-old has a hard time sharing. Sometimes he doesn't want anybody else to look at what he's looking at, sing the song he's singing, talk to the teacher he likes. Even if he's just finished admiring "his" dinosaur, singing "his" song, or playing with "his" teacher, that's all part of territory he claims and no other kid is supposed to enter.

In that museum situation, your inclination is to grab your child's hand, pull him toward the door, and tell him he's got to give somebody else a turn. You may get him moving, but probably not without a large fuss. And talking to him about taking turns will fall on deaf ears; children really don't get the idea of taking turns until they're between the ages of about 3 and 4.

A better approach:

> **"I know you had such a great time with this exhibit and game, you can't imagine somebody else touching it. But it really is here for other children as well."**

This will not necessarily make your child see the light and move peaceably aside, but he will appreciate that you know how he feels.

And then you will immediately point out and start talking about another nearby item of interest: "Let's try this one over here. It looks like fun." Usually, unless he's feeling superterritorial at the moment, your child will allow himself to be redirected. If he can't be persuaded and continues to push the new child away from "his" exhibit, you may just have to pick him up kicking and protesting and move on.

In some situations, consider if your child needs a little more of you. One 3-year-old was so possessive of his preschool teacher that his behavior was a classroom problem. He constantly pulled the teacher away from the other children, saying, "You have to be only for me." The boy's mother tried out 20 minutes a day of "floor time," giving her son her undivided attention and playing the games he wanted to play. Like a miracle, she says, the problem with his teacher stopped.

THE TOOLS: Empathize with your child's I-my-mine feelings. Offer substitutions. Spend some time each day doing just what he wants to do.

THROWS A TEMPER TANTRUM.

THE SCENE: While you're trying to get some grocery shopping accomplished, your child is amusing herself by tossing a grapefruit into the cart, then lifting up the back panel and watching the fruit plop to the ground. When you take the grapefruit away and tell her to cut it out, your child has a fit, a very loud fit. (Lots of tantrums happen in stores, by the way, because child *and* parent are tired and want to get out of there.)

THE BACKGROUND: Two- and 3-year-olds, and even some 4-year-olds, keep throwing tantrums at a full rate; that's a big part of the "terrible twos." Sometimes it can seem as if anything you say will set one off, but your child is not just trying to get your goat by being ornery. She's expressing her independence; she's trying to get something she needs. Or she may be tired or overstimulated at the moment. Or, possibly, she hasn't been getting enough parental attention lately.

Here's the good news: The 3-year-old tantrum can be a little easier to deal with than the 1½-year-old tantrum, because your child now has greater reasoning ability and a better grasp of time. That means you have more tools at your disposal.

Regarding the grocery store and the grapefruit, make it clear that your youngster can't do what she's doing, and offer a substitution:

> **"Fruit is not to be tossed around and played with. But you know what? We have to buy some toilet paper today, so let's go get that so you can throw those into the basket."**

A substitution *may* get you over the hump . . . or not. As said earlier, when nothing is working, abandon your shopping and leave for a while. Stay on your child's side.

One mother and her son David were walking home after a long afternoon of preschool and marketing. The boy demanded they stop in a doughnut shop they were passing, and when Mom said no he collapsed on the sidewalk, flailing and screaming in fury.

(A child's full-out, *public* temper tantrum is, of course, embarrassing in the extreme. Total strangers may feel free to comment, "What's the matter with him?" or give you disapproving looks. On the other hand, you might get a fellow parent passing by who gives you a smile and an eye roll that says, "I've been there. Don't worry, this too shall pass.")

Here's how David's mother coped:

Bending down close to her son, she said:

> "David, I know you're really angry and frustrated right now. We can't go in the doughnut shop. I'll stay here near you, but we're going to have to go home in another few minutes."

While he was carrying on, she stood quietly next to him, not meeting the eyes of passersby. Aware that she felt very angry, and pretty helpless too, she did some deep breathing to calm down and keep herself from doing or saying something she'd regret. After another minute of her child's kicking and screaming, she bent down again and said:

> "We'll be home soon and you can have some juice and then we'll think of something fun to do. But you do have to get up off the sidewalk and we do have to get moving here."

Finally, he settled down and stood up. His mom took him gently by the shoulder and said:

> "Let's run to the corner, and then we'll head home."

Although David was still squawky, he acquiesced.

THE TOOLS: When you must take something away, offer a substitution in its place; you may be able to head off a major tantrum. Your own emotions are running high while your child is throwing a tantrum; recognize your trigger points and spend a few moments calming <u>yourself</u> down.

Tell your child what's coming next and that things are going to get better—even if she doesn't know exactly what soon means, she's old enough to have heard you say this before and she knows you can be trusted to make things better. And if daily tantrums are making everybody's life miserable, give some thought to the kind of time you spend with your youngster. If you've been letting that 20 minutes of "floor time" go by the boards, get back to it.

WANTS TO EXPLORE EVERYTHING AND RUN, CLIMB, AND JUMP.

THE SCENE: You walk into the living room and, to your horror, see your 2¹/₂-year-old climbing up the front of the bookcase. Or, although he's generally pretty good about staying by your side, one afternoon he spots a friend down the street and darts off.

THE BACKGROUND: A child this age *has* to climb, run, and jump. Although he's more aware now than he was a year or a year and a half ago of possible dangers and of the wisdom of obeying Mom and Dad, his impulse control is still not great. The temptation to run, climb, and jump becomes greater than the desire to be safe and not get hurt; in fact, he will overcome obstacles in order to have the chance to run, climb, or jump. Plus, he's stronger and more capable than he was a while ago, which means he can get himself in even more precarious situations.

•   •   •

If your child is the monkey type who scales any upright
surface at the drop of a hat, you must, of course, first do
whatever is necessary to keep him safe. Anchor down the
bookcases or other tempting pieces of furniture. Store away
for the time being what can't be anchored. Make sure
window guards are strong and well secured. (But keep your
child away from windows in any case; children can climb
over guards.)

Then, provide him with lots of safe opportunities to climb,
on the playground equipment, on stepladders at home.

One 3-year-old just loved to jump. Every morning on
the walk to school he and his mom or dad passed a series
of low walls, and Garrett climbed up on every one and
jumped off. He jumped off the little wrought-iron guardrails
that ran around trees. And every afternoon he'd complain
that his legs hurt. His parents kept telling him to stop
jumping so much, but Garrett just couldn't stop himself.
One day his mom switched gears. Before they left for school,
she said:

> "You really like to jump off things. You do it
> every time we walk to school or walk home. I
> know it's fun to run and jump, and you don't
> like us telling you you can't do it. The problem
> is, it hurts your legs. Let's figure out how you
> can jump and not get hurt."

Garrett himself thought of the sandbox in the park, and said
he could jump off the edge into the sand. Mom said that was
a great idea, and they made a deal to stop at the park on the
way home that afternoon. She also suggested they put pillows
on the floor in the living room, and Garrett could jump from
the couch onto the pillows. He agreed not to jump off the
walls on the way to and from school.

THE TOOLS: Change "no" to "yes" and provide substitutions; while bookcases are off-limits, there are other, safer places to climb. When you're setting limits, involve your child in the solution (up to age 3½, remember that you'll have to come up with the solutions).

. . .

Two-and-a-half-year-old Eric and his mom were walking down a dock at a lake, when Eric suddenly wrenched free of his mother's hand, raced down the dock, and leaped into the water. His shocked mother jumped in after him and pulled up her sputtering and thrashing son. She told him how frightened she had been, what a dangerous thing he had done, and how important it was that he remember the rule about holding hands. When both had settled down a bit, she took Eric into the shallow part to play, so he wouldn't be afraid of the water after his experience. But 10 minutes later, Eric was dashing down the dock again. Mom chased after and caught him before he took another jump.

After calming herself with some deep breaths, she said:

> "Eric, I was absolutely terrified just now. You don't know how to swim yet, and we agreed that you have to hold my hand when we go on the dock but you just ran back again. I can't have you near the water for now."

She and Eric left the beach for 20 minutes, and Mom was able to tell him she appreciated how he felt:

> "I know it's exciting to see the other kids jumping in. We'll keep giving you swimming lessons so you'll be able to jump off the dock too. But until you've learned to swim better, you have to stay near me."

Her response to his behavior did the trick. When they returned to the beach, he played near her. On subsequent trips, he still liked going on the dock, but held his mother's hand.

THE TOOLS: To keep your child safe, <u>insist</u> he stay near you—no negotiating. If he does dash away, retrieve him from possible danger and impose a consequence: If he can't stay near you, he must leave the beach. Calm yourself down, but also let him know the impact of his behavior: What he did terrified you. And always, empathize and give him hope: You know it's so exciting to go jumping in the water, and someday he'll be able to do just that.

PUTS UP A FIGHT ABOUT BEDTIME.

THE SCENE: You finally have your 3-year-old down for the night. Or so you think. Although you gave in to the 20 more minutes playtime and the 10 more minutes in the bath and the one more book to be read, he's still demanding attention.

THE BACKGROUND: This one quickly drives parents to nagging, because after a long day you need quiet time for yourself. Your 3-year-old, on the other hand, is ready to keep going until he literally can't hold his eyes open, because there's so much to explore and going to bed puts an end to that. Sometimes, too, kids are going through a stage when they're fearful and need some more reassurance: Perhaps he's just moved into a big-boy bed or a sibling has encroached on his time. You may decide, therefore, not to insist he return to his room, and handle things a little differently.

Each evening, Allison's father read to her, which she loved. But Allison made an endless production of preparing for bed, dawdling about picking up toys, brushing teeth, getting into pajamas . . . and the reading sessions got later and later, despite her father's nagging her to keep moving. One night he quit the nagging; when they settled down to read, he said:

> Dad: **"Honey, we have ten minutes left for reading, so we only have time for this short book."**
> Allison: **"But, Daddy, you promised to read me three books."**
> Dad: **"I know I did, and I would love to read all three. But the time isn't available anymore, so we can't finish them. I hope we don't take so much time getting ready tomorrow and this doesn't happen again. We'll leave the other books right here for tomorrow night."**

Allison was not happy. She complained and cried for half an hour, but Dad didn't give in. Father and daughter went through the same scene for three nights in a row, and then abruptly the bedtime battles improved. This little girl's desire to spend cozy time reading with her dad outweighed her desire to protest, and she cut down on the dawdling.

THE TOOLS: Set your limits on what bedtime must be, and insist on them. Let her suffer the consequences of losing reading time if she can't get herself ready for bed fairly promptly. Give her hope that tomorrow things can go better, and give her a "yes" instead of a "no"—yes, we will read three books, just not tonight.

.   .   .

If your child is in a phase of repeatedly wandering out of his room, consider the possible reasons for it. One mother liked to end her day by getting into bed and reading or writing letters. Her son kept appearing in the doorway, looking forlorn. After many frustrating struggles, she said to him one evening:

> "This is my quiet time, but I see you're having trouble getting to sleep. You will have to be quiet, but I'll tell you what. You can bring your book in here and lie down at the end of my bed, and you can look at your book quietly. Maybe I'll fall asleep first or maybe you will."

Other evenings he was allowed to take his blanket and book into the living room and curl up on the floor next to his father while Dad was doing paperwork. After a couple of weeks of this routine, the boy felt comfortable settling into his own bed once again.

Another child held his father hostage in his bedroom, insisting he sit beside him until he fell asleep. Dad wanted this routine to stop. One evening he said:

> "Alex, I know you don't like falling asleep by yourself. I'm going to sit here for five minutes, and then I'm going in the other room because I need some time for myself. But I'll come back and check on you every ten minutes, and you'll see me."

He yelled and cried but the father persevered. He did what he promised, and in a few days his son was usually asleep by the time of the first "check-in."

Melissa's mother, a full-time working mom, faced huge battles with her 3-year-old over bedtime. Come nine o'clock,

ten o'clock, this youngster was not going to call it quits!
Finally, Mom made herself drop everything else that needed
attention when she first arrived home from work—dinner
and the mail and phone calls—and devoted an exclusive half
hour to her daughter, playing games the little girl devised.
Over time, Melissa's protests about bedtime died down
somewhat.

THE TOOLS: Empathize with your child's wish to have you
there while he's drifting off to sleep. At the same time, you
have your rights; you don't have to do <u>all</u> of what he wants.

Don't neglect the daily 20 or so uninterrupted minutes of
"floor time," especially if you've been away at work all day.
Bedtime struggles sometimes have a lot to do with the fact
that your child hasn't had enough of you.

DISLIKES BEING HURRIED.

THE SCENE: It's Saturday morning, you have half a dozen
errands to run, you have to take your 3-year-old along with
you . . . and you can't get her to budge.
THE BACKGROUND: It seems the more you're in a rush
to get moving the more your youngster is determined to slow
down. Around this age, your child is in a highly contrary
mode: She doesn't want to be told what to do! And she
doesn't want to be hurried.

You can say, "We're leaving now, you have one minute to
get your coat and meet me at the front door." That probably
will accomplish little and only make you both madder. You'll

have a better chance of achieving cooperation if you can convey to your child that the consequences of not hurrying now will be less time later to do something she wants to do, like have a play date with her friend or help you bake cookies. Say:

> "Diana, I know you want to have a play date with Ellen today. And it would be a lot more fun to do that than to go to the supermarket. But if we get these things done now, then they'll be over with and we won't have to worry about them anymore and you'll have more time to play this afternoon. So let's go do them."

Suppose Diana is still going nowhere. Move on to step two. Say:

> "If I wanted to go on a play date, I'd be unhappy, too, if somebody made me do errands instead. Let's think of how we can make it more fun for you. And I've got another idea. Let's call Ellen and you can talk to her before we leave, to be sure she'll be ready for the play date later."

If nothing is working, tell your child that you must leave, that she has to come along, and that you'll help her put on her coat if she wants. Getting her moving may involve some kicking and screaming and protesting on her part. Say:

> "I'm sorry we're both so unhappy, but we have to do this and I'll try to make it better for you. Maybe when you stop crying, you'll be able to figure out how to make it better too."

THE TOOLS: Give her some choices and some control; she can call her friend and feel in charge of what's going to happen later. Offer your regrets that she must do what she'd rather not do, while you make clear that it is going to happen. If you're getting into this situation a lot—you feeling rushed, your child feeling hurried—plan on spending more time working with her to gain cooperation.

IS RELUCTANT TO GIVE UP THE PACIFIER OR BOTTLE.

THE SCENE: Although he's almost 3, your child still demands his bottle first thing in the morning and last thing at night, and trying to talk him out of it turns into a power struggle.

THE BACKGROUND: By the time a child reaches this age, many parents become increasingly impatient with the bottle and the pacifier. But some youngsters require more sucking time than others, and perhaps feel especially needy when they're trying to relax, calm themselves down for sleep, or wake up to face a new day.

Wean your child off the bottle or pacifier in stages, and explain to him what's going to happen. Be honest and be respectful; don't have the pacifier suddenly and mysteriously get "lost" or talk about "big boys" versus "babies." Your youngster is likely to respond well to setting limits—he can have a bottle when he goes down for a nap but not at dinner, he can use his pacifier in the house but not outside, or whatever you decide.

One child who drank comfortably out of a cup during the day wouldn't settle down for sleep without his nighttime bottle of milk. His mother wanted to eliminate this final bottle, especially since her son's dentist expressed concern about damage to the boy's teeth. She said:

> "Philip, I know you like having your bottle when you go to bed at night, but Dr. Harris says it's not so good for your teeth. So here's what we can do. You can have no bottle or you can have your bottle with water in it. If you still want to have your bottle with water, I'll let you do that for a little while longer."

Philip wasn't too happy about the water, but he wasn't yet ready to give up his bottle entirely. Mom decided to let him have it for another month or so, and then try again to eliminate it entirely.

THE TOOLS: Ease your child off the bottle by presenting a compromise and offering a substitution. If you can, appoint a neutral bad guy—the dentist says this has to be done.

· · ·

A mother decided to allow her child to have a morning bottle, the one she really screamed for, and help her give up the others during the day. She put Erica's milk and juice into a sippy cup, and then allowed the little girl to snuggle up next to her while she drank. Erica resisted at first, but the nice snuggle time together was an encouragement. Mom also got a cup with Erica's name on it, for future use. She said:

> "You can drink from lots of things. Dad and I drink from cups and bottles and glasses, and you'll be drinking from these sometimes too. And this is going to be your cup, with your name on it. We'll keep this here for when you're ready to use it."

THE TOOLS: While you give a substitution, show your child you're on her side and you'll help her along. Tell her what comes next—eventually, she won't need her bottle anymore and it could be kind of fun to be drinking out of her very own cup.

.   .   .

One mother was driven batty by the sight of the omnipresent pacifier in her child's mouth. Although her son agreed that he'd no longer have the pacifier when they left the house, Mom wanted an end to it once and for all. She said:

> **"I think it's time we made a plan about no more pacifiers. What do you say we pick some day when you won't use it anymore?"**

They talked it over a bit, and Sean picked Christmas (a couple of months away) as D day. It worked. On Christmas Day, mother and son walked down the hallway of their apartment building to the trash chute and Sean himself tossed in his remaining stock of pacifiers.

THE TOOLS: Involve your child in the solution to giving up the bottle and the pacifier—youngsters this age really do know it's time to move on.

DOESN'T WANT HELP GETTING DRESSED.

THE SCENE: You're trying to get your squirming 2-year-old into her shirt, overalls, and socks and shoes. It feels as if you're engaged in a wrestling match.

THE BACKGROUND: Maybe she wants to get dressed by herself, she thinks she should be *able* to get dressed by herself, and she's getting madder and more frustrated by the minute because she can't find the sleeve hole or both legs ended up in one part of the pants.

When she's a little older and more capable of getting into and out of clothes, this kind of power struggle should die down (although there may be other reasons she's not in a mood to get dressed). Meantime, simplify the routine; encourage her to work on one aspect at a time. Say:

> **"It's tough to put that shirt on right, but you know what? You did a great job yesterday getting into your socks, so suppose you put on your socks and I'll put your shirt on for you."**

Give your youngster some power and control. She might not be so crabby about your helping her if she can pick whether she wants to wear the striped shirt or the blue one.

One father was in constant nagging scenes with his 3-year-old when it came time to get dressed. One day, he tried a different tack. In the evening, when everybody was calm and quiet, he said to his daughter:

> **"I can see you'd like to get all dressed in the morning without me helping you. And there are some things you're getting really good at and some things you have to practice some more. Let's make a list of all the things you can do for yourself in the morning."**

They came up with the list and Dad drew a chart with simple little stick figures showing what Janet could and would do—take off her pajamas, get her shirt and socks out of the drawer, close the Velcro clasps on her sneakers, put her jacket by the door, and so on. And Dad would take care of the rest. Janet felt pleased with herself for quite a few mornings afterward, and the struggles died down.

THE TOOLS: Offer your child choices; if she has some say in what she'll be wearing, she just might feel less overpowered and frustrated. Give her a little praise for what she <u>can</u> do, and a little hope for the future as well—one of these days, she'll be able to get dressed all by herself.

DOESN'T WANT TO SHARE A FAVORITE TOY.

THE SCENE: Your youngster insists on taking her toy motor scooter to the playground *and* insists that no one else can touch it. When other children reach for the scooter, she hits and shoves. Playtime degenerates into tears. She gets furious. You get upset with her.

THE BACKGROUND: Children this age are still in that "I, my, mine" stage; they usually get better at sharing and taking turns between ages 3 and 4. But any time a youngster owns a very special something, she's going to find it tough to turn it over to a playmate, even for a little while.

The father whose little girl would not let go of that motor scooter decided to talk to his child about the situation before they headed out to the playground one afternoon. He said:

> "Listen, you absolutely love this scooter, I know that. The problem is, every time we get to the playground everybody else wants to use it and you don't want them to get near it. So we just

> can't bring the scooter to the park unless you're
> able to let your friends try it sometimes."

Becky said she didn't want to do that. Dad replied:

> "Well, sweetie, then you're going to have to
> leave it at home, and I promise your mom and I
> will find plenty of other times and places you can
> ride it. But we can't bring it to the playground
> and not have you allow someone else to take a
> turn with it, because you know what always
> happens. You've seen what happens."

Becky went off and thought about the situation for a while,
and then told her dad she'd changed her mind. She did want
to take the scooter and she could share it. Her father said:

> "Are you sure? Because if we get to the park
> with it and you can't let the other kids have a
> turn, we're going to have to leave. So I want to
> be sure you understand that we can either leave
> it home, because I know you don't want anybody
> else to use it, or we can bring it with us and
> you'll share it."

He stuck by his guns. If things went badly at the playground,
he was prepared to take Becky home. The little girl did what
she had said she would do, and her father let her know later
on that he felt really happy when he saw Becky sharing her
scooter. He said:

> "I felt terrific when I saw what you were doing.
> That little boy who had a turn on your scooter
> looked so happy. I was really pleased with you, that
> you were able to give it a try and that it worked."

THE TOOLS: Empathize. It really is <u>very</u> hard for youngsters this age to share the toys they love. Include your child in the decision-making, let her make a choice. Set limits and make the consequences clear. And praise her for a job well done by describing the impact her behavior had on you and on other people (that happy little playmate).

WON'T SIT STILL AT THE TABLE.

THE SCENE: You've coaxed your son to come in to dinner. He sits at the table for thirty seconds, then races off, grabbing a piece of chicken from his plate on the way.

THE BACKGROUND: Maybe your child finds dinnertime a bit boring, because Mom and Dad tend to leave him out of the conversation. Maybe he knows that dinner signals the day is coming to a close, and he wants to get in one last round of play—even 2-year-olds have their agendas. And maybe his attention span is really pretty short.

Start by sending your child sufficient alerts:

> "Frankie, dinner will be ready soon. You have enough time to finish up that puzzle and wash your hands."
>
> "Okay, two more minutes now. We're having macaroni and chicken and chocolate pudding, and you're going to like it."

You may get him primed to come in for dinner, and still not be able to keep him there for long. Go after him and let him know he's expected to eat:

> "I know you don't feel like sitting at the table, but now it's time for dinner. When you leave the kitchen, I think you're finished and I should take your plate away, but I know you're hungry so please come back and have something to eat."

While he's sitting down with the family, make an effort to talk more to him—skip some of the grown-up conversation; tell a story that's sure to amuse him or engage his attention.

Your best bet is to figure out ahead of time what measure of compliance you can reasonably expect, and think of ways to promote it. Maybe, for example, you'd like him sitting still for 20 minutes but 5 is all he seems to manage before getting antsy. Before your next meal, tell him the plan. Say:

> "I know it's the hardest thing for you to sit down and stay there. But Mom and I love having you with us at dinner. So let's agree you'll sit with us for five minutes, and then you can get down and play quietly nearby for a little while. And then maybe you'll come back later and finish your meal."

If you can, share your own experiences with him:

> "If I didn't want to sit still, I might not do what I was told either. Sometimes when I go to a business dinner with Mom and I'm not interested in what everybody's talking about, I feel like getting up and going for a walk outside!"

You should be able to get him at the table for some of the meal, and at least prevent him from running around the house with a chicken leg in his hand.

THE TOOLS: Tell him what to expect and provide transitions; he'll settle into a mealtime mood more easily if he has enough warning and chances to end his play. Empathize—tell him you know it's hard to sit still, because you find it hard sometimes yourself. Tell him the impact of his behavior—he makes his parents happy when he joins them for dinner. Keeping reasonable expectations in mind, compromise, and involve him in a solution so you each get some of what you want.

WON'T EAT THE DINNER SERVED.

THE SCENE: You've been having a running battle over dinner for the last two weeks. Your 3-year-old thinks everything you serve is icky and doesn't want any part of it.
THE BACKGROUND: Children really do want to eat, for the simple reason that they don't like being hungry. But they also like to have some say in what they get to eat, just as you and I do.

If these food wars are becoming entrenched in your household, at the beginning of the week, sit down with your child and say:

> "I know you love macaroni and cheese, and you also like hamburgers and those french fries in the frozen packages. You're going to be able to have those things twice a week . . . and you can pick what days you'd like them and let's mark them down right here on the calendar. We'll go to the supermarket this afternoon and you can pick those things out. And I'll pick out some other foods that Dad and I like to eat, and we'll have those on the other days."

THE TOOLS: Respect your child's wishes. Empathize. Say "yes"—you can have what you want sometimes. Offer choices. Set up a little success story; help her see that she can contribute to the smooth running of the family.

. . .

SCENE TWO: (food struggles, continued) You've served up the hamburgers and fries on Wednesday, per your child's request, and she says they're icky and wants no part of dinner. **MORE BACKGROUND:** Sometimes (especially around ages 2½ and 4½) children enter a particularly defiant stage and dig in their heels. Or maybe your youngster just isn't hungry or maybe she's feeling cranky about something else. Say:

> **"I'm sorry, honey, but this is the meal you picked and this is it for tonight. We'll have something else tomorrow, and maybe you'll like that better."**

Maybe she'll eat dinner, maybe she won't. If she doesn't eat, give her milk or juice before she goes to bed so she won't become dehydrated . . . but there's nothing wrong with letting her feel a little hungry. You're not a short-order cook, and you've been a cooperative parent by serving her requests.

THE TOOLS: Express your regrets. Impose appropriate consequences (you don't eat, you get hungry). Give her hope (maybe tomorrow's dinner will make her happier).

LOSES INTEREST IN TOILET TRAINING.

THE SCENE: Although your youngster was doing pretty well using the potty for a while, suddenly he won't go near it anymore.

THE BACKGROUND: You're probably pretty relaxed about toilet training if your child is 2 or 2½; you know the deed will get accomplished eventually. When he's still not toilet trained by age 3 or older—and *especially* if he seemed to be making headway, but then lost interest—you may start to get annoyed or concerned and on his case.

There are many reasons a child may become disinterested in the potty, none of them very serious. Maybe he feels pressured to perform, or he wants to stay "the baby" in the family, or once the novelty of using the potty wears off it's a nuisance to interrupt his play to get to the bathroom.

Stay relaxed. Just stop having an argument about it.

One 3-year-old who had been using the potty started to squat in the corner and have a BM in her pants. Her mom kept urging her during the day and especially before they left the house, "Let's go to the bathroom first. Let's give it a try. That's what big girls do," and so on. One day, she switched gears. She said:

> "For now, it looks like you want to go in your pants instead of using the potty. I know you will use the potty one day, because everybody does. But I think you're just not ready for this, and I'm not even going to ask you about it for the next three weeks."

And she didn't. During that time, Mom and Dad both let their child observe them using the toilet, so she would see that's what people do. And before they went out, Mom or Dad would sometimes remark, "I'm going to go to the bathroom before we leave, so I don't get caught when we're in the park." But they left their daughter alone, and made no more references to being a "big girl." After about a month of this approach, the girl walked into the bathroom by herself and was back on the potty.

Another 3-year-old, after several successful weeks using the potty every night, abruptly changed his mind about toilet training. Mom said:

> **"You know, I would like you to use the potty, but it looks like you don't want to right now. I know in time you will use it."**

Both parents let the matter drop for several weeks, until Chris was about to enter a summer day camp where some of the activities—going in the wading pool or under the sprinkler— required he be toilet trained. Mom said:

> **"Chris, you will need to be using a potty if you want to go swimming or under the sprinkler at camp. And those are fun things that I know you like doing."**

This observation failed to turn things around, but Chris's parents plan to remind him again once camp gets closer. He may be motivated to return to the potty; if he's not, he won't be able to swim.

THE TOOLS: Give your child hope—tell him you know he'll be able to handle this someday. Plan a joint approach with your spouse—you'll set the situation back if one of you is nagging your youngster to perform, but you'll help him go forward if he sees that Mom and Dad both do believe in using the toilet! Don't push, but if he does keep refusing he may have to suffer the consequences of not using the potty, like not being able to go swimming.

————

WHEN YOUR
3- TO
4-YEAR-OLD . . .

RESISTS LEAVING A PLAY DATE.

THE SCENE: Your 4-year-old, having a grand time at her friend's house, refuses to leave when you come to pick her up. You give her 10 more minutes, and then an additional 10 minutes, and still she's not going anywhere.

THE BACKGROUND: Children this age can become emboldened in their stubbornness when they're in someone else's house and have a playmate for an ally. And you're feeling really irked, because you've been nice, you've given her some transition time, and now this has all the looks of escalating into a major row.

Say:

> "I know you're having a great time and you hate to leave and you're mad at me for making you leave. I don't blame you. I don't like to leave either when I'm having a good time. But we do have to go now, so get your coat on and remember your backpack."

Your child still balks:

> "I don't want to go. Melissa wants me to stay. Why can't I stay? Why do we have to go right now?"

You say:

> "I can see this is hard for you, but we have to go. Let's pick a date right now for the two of you to get together again."

THE TOOLS: Empathize. Offer your regrets over her unhappiness. Change "no" to "yes," by telling her when she can play again.

. . .

Despite your efforts, perhaps your child resumes playing with her friend. You say:

> "Honey, I understand this is tough on you, but it's time for us to move on. Do you want to get your coat and things, or should I get them for you and get you ready? You decide."

Usually the struggle ends at this point and the child decides to dress herself.

What if she still ignores you? Get her coat, put it on her, and start moving out. How annoyed you are at this point can easily affect whether you are able to try another step, but if you're game enough to soldier on, here's what to do.

Ask her:

> **"What would make it easier for you to leave? You tell me."**

And then perhaps she will make some final demand—she wants you to carry the backpack and she absolutely won't put on her coat until you get outside. You say:

> **"Well, sure, that's okay by me."**

And then you pick up her bag and head for the door. It's tempting, at such a point, to lose patience. You may think, I don't like the way this kid is talking to me, after I've bent over backward to be nice. And then you may be tempted to say, "I think you can carry your own bag and put your coat on *now*." That would be a mistake.

THE TOOLS: Empathize some more. Give your child a real choice, and let her save face. She is relinquishing some independence and going along with you, but she wants to have the last word. Let her have it.

DAWDLES.

THE SCENE: You've reminded your 3½-year-old that it's almost time to leave for gym class. Twenty minutes later she's still in her underwear, painstakingly lining up all her stuffed animals on the windowsill.

THE BACKGROUND: Like a younger child, a 3- to 4-year-old doesn't want to be hurried. And chances are, even if the next item on the agenda is something she regularly enjoys, she may be totally absorbed in another captivating activity and have no wish to abandon it—she's just having too much fun.

Sometimes, too, a child drags her feet and dawdles because she'd rather have a little more of you for the moment.

Suppose you remind your youngster yet again that you've got to be on your way to her gym class and she announces she'd like you to read her a book—right now. If she really does always like gym class, you can assume that she's making a plea for you to spend more time with her. Say:

> "I know you'd like to stay home and have me read to you. It's upsetting that we don't have more time to spend together right now, but you know you'll have fun at gym."

And then she might reply:

> "Read me the book!"

It's time for a little negotiation. Say:

> "I'll tell you what. When you start getting on your clothes, I'll read the book out loud. And then you have gym to go to and I have work to do. If it's getting too late, we'll finish half the book now and the other half tonight. And we can do some more reading then too."

THE TOOLS: Negotiate and give in a little—you'll do some of what she wants and she'll do some of what you want. That's also changing a "no" to a "yes." Give her information about what's going to happen and some hope: She'll go to her class and you'll go to work, and then the lovely evening will come when she can have you and her books all to herself!

.   .   .

Here's another common dawdling scene: You and your child are heading down the street, off to run an errand or visit a friend. You're walking slowly enough, you think; she's walking at a maddening snail's pace, causing you to stop every five feet and wait. When she catches up, take her hand and say:

> "I have to insist you walk a little faster. I'm really sorry because I know you want to walk slowly and look at everything along the way. But if we don't get going, we'll be late and you won't have much time later to play."

THE TOOLS: Offer your regrets that she's got to get hustling when she'd rather dawdle. Let her know the consequences: It will work to her benefit if she goes along with your demand.

DISLIKES ROUTINES.

THE SCENE: Your 3-year-old has his regular chores—to help put groceries away on a low shelf, bring plates into the kitchen after dinner, and lay out the clothes he's going to wear the next morning. He's good about doing the chores— he feels very important about them, in fact—until one day, suddenly, he doesn't want to do them anymore. He also resists his regular bathtime and bedtime rituals and even his favorite crackers/milk/rest time afternoon routine.

THE BACKGROUND: Very young children *need* routines, and want them. Routines help them to feel comfortable and secure and to learn about time. Routines also, as any parent knows, are what keep chaos and confusion to a minimum in the household. When they reach the age of 3 or 4, however, children often suddenly get tired of those familiar routines. They want to do things differently.

If your child starts balking at doing his chores, you can remind him of what's expected. Say:

> "My job here is to cook the meal and remember what your job is. Your job is to bring the plates into the kitchen after dinner so they can get washed."

If reminders don't work, he's probably just tired of doing the same things. Find some new ones: Ask him if he'd like to change jobs and instead, unload the spoons and forks from the dishwasher, or fold washcloths that come out of the laundry.

A mother of two boys, ages 3½ and 7, had come to dread the nightly bathtimes. One or the other of her sons feuded over having a bath in the first place—then, once in the tub, wouldn't get out and splashed water all over. At a parenting session, we suggested she change her approach; first, she'd discuss the problem at a time other than bathtime. She said:

> "I know you guys both hate baths, but you still need to be clean. So let's see how we can make it easier for you. I think it would be okay if you have a bath every other day, not every night."

They liked that idea. She then asked:

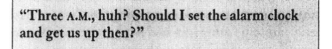

"We have to pick a time and stick to it. When do you want to do your baths?"

The boys said they'd have their baths at three A.M. Mom jokingly went along:

"Three A.M., huh? Should I set the alarm clock and get us up then?"

They laughed and said no, then decided that on some nights they'd be willing to have the bath at six-thirty and some nights at seven-thirty. And so they did. This mother said that after two months of nonstop stress over the bath issue, the entire problem was settled within a couple of days. The boys still sometimes complained, but when Mom said, "Well, should we do it a different way?" they said no and complied with the agreement.

THE TOOLS: Decide which routines really must be maintained and you must insist on—you have to stick with bedtime and morning drills, if the household is to keep running smoothly. Then introduce a little variety into the routines that can be changed.

Be empathetic and, to the extent that it's possible, be willing to negotiate and compromise: You can skip a bath every other night and you can pick the time you'll have it. Involve your child in the solution. And a little humor while you're negotiating can make things run more smoothly.

EXCLUDES OR IS EXCLUDED BY OTHER CHILDREN AT PLAY.

THE SCENE: Your normally sunny 4-year-old starts coming home from preschool looking glum . . . and proceeds to make the rest of your afternoon together unpleasant by demanding attention with lots of whining and crankiness. After several days of this and some gentle questioning from you, she tells you Tessa and some other girl said her barrette was funny-looking and she couldn't play with them anymore.

THE BACKGROUND: We tend to think cliques, with the hurtful behavior that causes misery for the excluded child, start rearing up in the middle of the middle school years—among fifth and sixth graders. In fact, $3^1/_2$-, 4-, and 5-year-olds can be very good at ousting someone from the group, usually at the instigation of one child who's "the boss" and often ostensibly because of some minor "infraction," like wearing the wrong barrette.

If your child has been singled out for rejection, helping her through it will take great patience. The trouble will go away, but not overnight. Start by saying:

> "I know it's terrible when kids don't want to play with you, especially when they say something silly like your barrette looks funny. We know there's nothing wrong with your barrette. And you know what else? I think that Tessa must not be feeling very good about herself if she has to say things like that. But it still feels terrible. I hated it when that happened to me when I was little and someone left me out. We'll have to find a way to make things better while this is going on."

Since young children will think Mom or Dad can solve all problems, your child may insist you go and tell that other girl she has to play with her. You can say:

> "If they keep saying you can't play, I can talk to Tessa's parents, and I will do that, but things may not change right away. Let's think of what else we can do. We'll make some play dates with kids you haven't seen much of—you tell me who we should invite over. And I can talk to your teacher. Maybe the teacher can set you up in another part of the room where there's somebody who'll definitely want to play with you. We'll make sure you have a lot of good times."

Then do what you said. It's never easy to approach another parent whose child is making yours miserable; you'll have the greatest chance of success if you bring up the matter with understanding and in a nonthreatening tone: "It's hard to believe these little kids are excluding people, but my daughter is being left out of the group and I just thought if there's something you could say to Tessa to try to make things easier, that would be great." You may not accomplish much, but you can tell your daughter you tried.

As the rejection goes on, your child will be unhappy and remind you that "the boss" is still being mean to her. Let her know you appreciate all that, and help her focus on what's going on right at the moment. Say:

> "I know, and we've got to assume that she's just full of herself for now if she keeps on being mean to you. But tell me, how has it been going when Carolyn comes over?"

If you've been masterminding those play dates, chances are she'll tell you cheerfully that she and Carolyn have been having lots of fun and she also wants to invite Erin to come and play. And chances are the leader of the clique will lose her power over time, and the rejection will stop.

THE TOOLS: If ever a child's problem demanded parental empathy, this is it. It's so painful for a child to be excluded by her peers, and that's a pain most of us can remember vividly from our own youth. Letting her know that you know just how she feels really helps.

And let her know what she can expect—things are not going to be better right away, but here are the steps we'll take to get there. Get her to participate in the solution—by making play dates, for example.

. . .

Three-year-old Mary had two little friends in her home for a play date; she and one boy played and left the other girl out. Mary's mother was aware of what had gone on, and after the children left said to her daughter:

> "Sally looked very sad today. She felt no one cared about her. How do you think you'd feel if you went to Sally's house and she played with someone else and left you out? It really feels terrible to be left out."

Mary looked down at the floor and said, "Okay." And in fact, that was enough to correct the problem the next time the three friends got together.

Let's say Mary continued to exclude. Her mother would then need to impose a consequence. She might say:

> "We can't have one of your friends left out when she comes here. We talked about that before. Maybe for a couple of days it would be better for you to play on your own."

Mom might also try to find out if her child is getting this kind of treatment herself in another group. Or, she might need to end threesomes for a while.

THE TOOLS: Let her know the impact of her behavior: She's making somebody else feel very unhappy. Parents worry about making a child feel guilty and bad about herself. But I distinguish between good guilt and bad guilt. Saying to a young child who's a picky eater, "You make me feel very sad when you don't eat" is imposing bad guilt. Saying, "You really hurt your friend's feelings when you treated her that way" is good guilt; it promotes sensitivity and good action. Impose a consequence for her behavior: no play dates for a while.

HAS FEARS.

THE SCENE: On a warm, sunny spring day you take your 3-year-old to the park, anticipating an enjoyable afternoon riding the carousel. But when you get there, your child wants no part of those horses going around and around, hangs on to your leg, and can't be persuaded to get anywhere near the action.

THE BACKGROUND: When a child reaches age 3, 4, and 5, he's turning into a powerful, aware little person; he's able to do a lot more than he used to, he's physically stronger, he can wonder what's going to happen, he can see that a lot of the world can't be under his control. And from time to time, that scares him. It's common for a child at these ages to fear animals, movies, bedtime, the dark, loud sounds, clowns, disabled people, or any number of other objects or circumstances that make him feel less in control. He might respond by acting timid or withdrawn *or* like a supertough guy.

Parents tend to feel uncomfortable about a child's fearfulness, and try to jolly him out of it by telling him there's nothing to be afraid of. Usually, what that child needs is empathy and time.

For example, that youngster at the carousel is probably worrying about how he'll hold on to the horse, when it will stop, and how he'll get off. Give him the time to watch, with no urging on from you. Stand with him clutching your leg for 20 minutes or as long as it takes; when he sees how a carousel works, he may want to give it a try. If he doesn't, come back another day.

If your child gets upset every time he sees a dog approaching, anticipate his fear. Say:

> **"I know you're worried about that dog. We can go over to the other side of the street and that dog won't come near."**

A mother in one of my groups told a story that shows how a child may act aggressively in response to fear. She and her 4-year-old son were exploring a children's zoo and passed a display tank containing an immense boa constrictor. Looking at the snake, Paul began jumping around and yelling, "I'm going to kick your butt!" and other tough-guy talk.

His mother recognized that Paul was probably afraid ("I'm terrified of snakes myself and I don't want him to be too," she told us), and said: "Oh, come on, Paul, you're not afraid of that snake, it can't hurt you." Paul started shouting even louder. And then, said Paul's mother a bit ruefully, a nearby mother demonstrated a better way. The woman said to Paul:

> **"That's a really big, creepy snake, isn't it? It's bigger than you and me."**

Paul settled down, looked at the boa constrictor, and said, "I'm scared of that snake."

Said the woman:

> **"A lot of people are afraid of snakes. I don't like them much myself. I'm glad it's behind the glass, aren't you?"**

Paul said he was very glad, and soon Paul and his mother moved on quietly. Clearly, once his fear was out on the table, he didn't feel so afraid.

THE TOOLS: Empathize—let your child know you understand how he feels, and don't tell him or imply by your actions that he's wrong, babyish, or silly to feel that way. And remember: Overcoming fears takes time.

GOES WILD IN THE CAR.

THE SCENE: You're driving your 4-year-old and three of his schoolmates home from a school outing and the noise inside your car is deafening. Wrestling matches are breaking out in the backseat. Small paper and plastic objects are flying into the front seat.

THE BACKGROUND: When your child is older, you may find that some of the best conversations between the two of you happen while you're driving him someplace. Many parents discover there's something about the movement of the car, music on the radio, and limited eye contact that make a child feel comfortably chatty and even revelatory. While he's still part of the 5-and-under crowd, however, car rides usually make a child feel restless, bored, and in a mood to act up.

If you're on a long haul, be prepared to stop after about an hour and let kids run around. They simply can't sit still for that long, even with all the audiotapes in the world. Do have the tapes ready, though, along with snacks, plastic bottles of water, lots of napkins, trash bags in the backseat, and neat car games (the ever-popular "I spy with my little eye," for example) in mind to play. But when kids get really rambunctious, you've got to call a halt.

Say:

> **"Your noise is making it difficult for me to concentrate. I must have more quiet for us to be safe. This is important. If you can't settle down, I'll have to pull over to the side of the road."**

If the noise continues, do just that. Pull over, turn off the engine, *say nothing* (no negotiating, no explaining, no yelling), and sit there for several minutes.

THE TOOLS: When it comes to health, safety, and the law, you're the boss. You can't tolerate wild behavior in the car, not only because it's annoying but because it has an impact on how safely you are able to drive. Pulling over and remaining there quietly shows you mean business, as a consequence to their behavior, and the noise will subside.

· · ·

One father had difficulty taking his toddler in a taxi. As soon as the cab took off, the youngster climbed up on the seat to look out the back window and began jumping up and down. Now when this happens, Dad pulls his child down and constrains her firmly for the rest of the ride, over his daughter's protests.

Later, he says:

> **"I'm sorry I had to hold you so tightly. I know you don't like that, but there's no jumping in taxis and that's the only way I can be sure you don't get hurt."**

THE TOOLS: Make the consequences clear—you jump, you get held down. Empathize and share your regrets—"You don't like me holding you, I know, and I'm sorry I have to do that."

GETS OVEREXCITED.

THE SCENE: A couple of your child's friends have come over for an afternoon of play, and the scene is getting rowdier and rowdier. Kids are shrieking and racing through the house; you're doing a lot of shouting yourself, trying to get them settled down.

THE BACKGROUND: Two youngsters can start getting wild. Three or more can quickly reach critical mass, as they pump up each other's energy, get overstimulated or overtired and out of control. And by this age they can run! Your child is also likely to get overexcited when you go visiting another family and the anticipation has wound her up, when the weekend is coming to an end, and at holiday times from all the bustle and festivity.

Safety is your first concern: Wound-up kids are in danger of hurting themselves.

At her party, one little girl had dumped her shoes and was careening around in socks on the mostly bare floors. Her mom told her she had to put the sneakers back on, or she was going to slip. Said her daughter, dashing off: "No sneakers!" Mom caught her and said:

> "Here's your choice. You can wear only your socks and stay in your room. Or you can put on your sneakers and play out here with your friends. You pick!"

The daughter struggled and protested; Mom held on and repeated the drill. Then the child put on her shoes and played with her pals.

Getting a group of hypercharged, partying 4-year-olds to settle down takes energy and attention and possibly some ringmaster skills. Anticipate bedlam and be ready to switch to some quiet games or activities—for example, stretch a roll of blank newsprint or brown wrapping paper down a hallway and let youngsters lie on the floor drawing murals with crayons or markers.

As soon as two young brothers arrived for a visit with family friends, they demanded to know what games were available, talking in loud voices and generally taking over the scene. Their mother threatened them with leaving if they didn't behave. But the father who was the host recognized that the boys were overexcited *and* had been cooped up during a fairly long car ride, and he saw a better way to get them settled down. He said:

> "I know you guys have been really looking forward to this visit and you've been stuck in that car for a long time. There's still some time before it gets dark out, so we're going to move this whole party out to the backyard and you kids can play outside."

Everybody went out, and after half an hour or so of running around and letting off some steam, the youngsters were more amenable to direction and settled down inside to blocks and Candy Land. One of the adults was assigned to supervise the kids on a periodic basis, and all went smoothly.

THE TOOLS: Put a stop to running wild, if necessary by physically grabbing your child to keep her safe. Offer a choice:

Act wild and stay in your room, or calm down and join the party. Be empathetic: It <u>is</u> hard to be stuck in a car. Be a play date supervisor: Orchestrate activities to help kids get themselves out of the manic mode and settled down. If at all possible, get in some outdoor time so children can enjoy the fresh air and work off pent-up energy.

WANTS EVERYTHING HE SEES.

THE SCENE: You and your 3½-year-old have gone to your local Toys "R" Us to pick up a birthday present for his friend, and your youngster has a severe attack of the gimmes. You don't see how to leave the store without buying him a toy or getting into a major tantrum scene. This has happened before. And, once again, you resent being badgered into doing something that doesn't feel right and that you think will spoil your child.
THE BACKGROUND: We all love getting treats, but 3- and 4-year-olds have a particularly hard time delaying gratification. Going into a toy store—especially when you're there to pick out a gift for someone else!—is just too enticing. If you usually give in, you may have more of a struggle next time, but you can break the pattern.

Here's how one mother helped her child get over the gimmes:

As she and her little boy shopped for a birthday gift for his classmate Wendy, he announced he didn't like shopping for girls because he didn't like girl stuff. Mom saw where this argument was heading. She said:

> "I know it's more fun to look at boy's stuff and things that you'd like to have. I like to buy things for myself, too. But you know, if I were shopping for you, I'd look for something you'd like. Now we're looking for Wendy and I think she'd like this bear. I know you'd probably like an attack cat better."

Child:

> "Yes, and I know another store where they have
> them, so can't we go there?"

Mom:

> "Right now I have enough money to buy a
> present for Wendy and a little left over, but not
> enough for an attack cat. But you know,
> Christmas is coming up soon and we can put
> that on your wish list."

Her little boy wasn't thrilled with that suggestion. She tried again:

> "It looks like I'm going to leave here without
> anything! Couldn't you look in your pockets and
> see if you have any more money?"

Mom:

> "I know it's hard to go to a store and see so many
> neat things. It happens to me when I walk by
> that shoe store on our corner and I see so many
> shoes I'd like to have. But it's okay to want
> something, and it's nice to think about when you
> might be able to get it."

Mom stuck by her guns, and mother and son left that store with only the birthday gift they had come for. Two days later, they went to the shop that carried the desired attack cat and Mom asked the clerk to put one on reserve. The little boy said to the clerk, "I can't buy it right now. It's on my wish list."

Even if there's no special occasion coming up, such as

Christmas or your child's birthday, consider if it would be reasonable, and within your budget, to pick up a new toy. You might say:

> **"I'm just thinking, you haven't had a new toy in quite a while. You're due for one. We're not going to get something today, but on Saturday we'll go shopping and we'll see what we can get for you."**

It's appropriate that children be told what portion of the family resources is available to them. One mother and father told their two children each could have a "monthly toy" for about ten dollars (that amount, of course, might be two dollars or five dollars or whatever the budget will allow). When they were still very little, the youngsters always selected a toy each month; by the time they reached age 5, and were better able to postpone gratification, they'd often put two months' allotments together to buy something bigger and better.

These parents felt their ten-dollar-a-month approach was fair to the children, helped with their beginning knowledge of budgets, and contributed to their sense of control over their lives. And Mom and Dad were able to set clear limits and reduce the nagging for toys.

THE TOOLS: When your child wants what he sees and you must deny his entreaties, empathize: Tell him you <u>know</u> how hard it is not to get something he wants, because the same thing happens to you. Give him hope for the future, and you help him learn that although something isn't possible today it may be tomorrow. And then stick by your decisions even if he continues to protest.

WON'T GET DRESSED.

THE SCENE: You've told your 4-year-old, more than once, that it's almost time to leave for school and she'd better get dressed. Nothing is happening.

THE BACKGROUND: A 2-year-old wants to put her clothes on all by herself, but she can't manage it and often gets frustrated. A 4-year-old is *able* to do it, but often just won't . . . because she's playing and doesn't want to stop, or she's not in the mood to leave home and move on to the next item on the agenda, or she doesn't like Mom or Dad bossing her around. And some kids get fussy and dawdly about *what* they'll wear.

A child's refusal to get dressed seems to rank right up there with refusing to pick up toys as a major parent-child battle. Many parents in my workshops say getting their youngster dressed and out in the morning is their biggest headache.

One mother who got caught up in nagging changed her approach one morning. She went into her daughter's room and said:

> **"Tell me what you're going to do to help us get downstairs for breakfast."**

The little girl said, "I'm going to put on my pants and my sweatshirt." She did, and then went in the kitchen for breakfast. Her mom, somewhat amazed, says they haven't had getting-dressed problems since. Clearly, her child liked the idea that she could make things better and that she wasn't going to be simply wrenched from her room at Mom's command.

When you've been getting nowhere, you might also say:

> **"We need to leave, you need to get your clothes on. I've asked you several times. Now we have to get this done in ten minutes. Who's going to dress you, you or me?"**

If she says she'll do it, set a timer to help her along. If the timer dings and still no clothes are on, put them on for her, even if she protests. Next time around, see if you can allow more time for her to get the job done.

Here's another approach:

> **"You know you have to get dressed and that's not happening. Talk to me about why you're not getting ready. Do you know why you won't get dressed?"**

Your child may tell you she wants to keep playing or she doesn't feel like going to ballet class. Listen to her reasons; honor them if they make sense, but let her know that you'll be making the final decision about if and when you're leaving. Or she may not give an answer at all. But if instead of overpowering her you ask, "What's holding things up?" she does see that you're trying to understand and you don't just think she's being an ornery kid. In the long run, that helps.

THE TOOLS: **Get your child involved in solutions and offer choices—you can get this done or I'll get it done for you. Provide transitions—I'll come back in 10 minutes and then we'll see where we are.**

WON'T PICK UP TOYS.

THE SCENE: The floor of your 3-year-old's room is strewn with toys. In fact, blocks, crayons, plastic animals, and seemingly every plaything your child owns cover many surfaces in your house, and although you've told her to start picking up she's not doing it.

THE BACKGROUND: She's having a fine time, and doesn't want to move along to bed or something equally not much fun. Even if she's finished playing, what's the big deal, she thinks, about putting toys away? And, of course, she's testing her autonomy by ignoring your requests for cleanup.

Getting a child to gather her toys and tidy up is a very common, very annoying parent-child battle. It's an issue that comes up repeatedly in my workshops. Those little kids just don't want to comply . . . and after three reminders, Mom or Dad is solidly in nagging mode. A parent in one group said: "I want to yell, 'Clean it up! *Right now!* Or you're getting a time-out!' "

Avoid that kind of head-on collision, and you'll get more accomplished. Suppose coloring books and art supplies are scattered over the kitchen table. Instead of "Pick up your books," say:

> **"Your books and markers are covering up the table and I'm going to need that space in a few minutes, so you'll have to take those things away."**

Your child's room is littered with toys. Instead of "It's time to get all this stuff put away," you might say:

> **"Whoa, this room is a mess! It's so crowded in here I can't even find a place to sit down. Remember we were going to play Memory later, but we haven't got any place to play."**

THE TOOLS: Show her that her actions have an impact on you—you can't set the table for dinner, you can't find room to sit down. And if she <u>doesn't</u> take the action of picking up, that's going to have consequences for her—dinner is late or not so pleasant, because the kitchen was cluttered, or she can't go on to have a game with you.

.   .   .

Here's another way to foster cooperation. Survey the toy-strewn room and say:

> "Okay, we need to get this placed picked up. What part do you want to do? Do you want to put away the people and the horses or do you want to pick up the blocks and I'll take care of the people and the horses?"

Giving your child a choice of job is likely to get her going. If it doesn't, take another step. Say:

> "You know, you wanted to play with all these things and now you'll have to put them away. That's how we do things in this house. I'll give you a little time to work on this, and you can call me if you want my help."

Then give her that time. A child often requires a few minutes to come around to the point of doing what she knows she must do. If you return and see nothing has happened, say:

> "All these toys do have to be put away now. I'm going to get started and you can help me. But you know, it isn't right for someone else to pick up your things, especially when that person wasn't even playing with them. Tomorrow you can choose one or two things to play with, but you can't get out all these toys."

And the next day, stick with the consequences you imposed.

THE TOOLS: Involve your child in the solution by giving her a choice of tasks. Allow a little time for the message to sink in. Impose consequences: "Since you didn't do a great job at cleanup, next time you'll have to play with fewer things so we don't have so much to tidy up."

. . .

A mother who often got into arguments with her daughter about picking up toys and clothes decided to try a different tack one evening. She made up a story:

> "Once upon a time there was a little girl named Monica who loved to play. She took out one toy, then she wanted another toy, then another toy, and pretty soon there were toys all over the place. Boy, what a pile of stuff and what a messy room!"

The story got elaborate, with various twists and turns about how those toys got put away, and even included a spider who put four pairs of Monica's shoes on his eight legs and walked them into the closet. Monica was charmed, although not a whole lot of tidying up got done that night. For several days afterward, however, says Monica's mom, the little girl was much more cooperative at cleanup time.

THE TOOLS: Get dramatic; use a little humor to make your point. And remember that behavior corrections can be spread out, because your child is still there the next day. You may not get an instant response, but find matters improve later.

HAS TROUBLE SHARING.

THE SCENE: You've taken your 3¹/₂-year-old and his best friend to the circus, and your child is nibbling at a huge box of popcorn. The friend says, "Can I have some?" Your child says, "No."

THE BACKGROUND: When he was in his "I, my, mine" stage, around age 2, your child didn't grasp the notion of sharing.

Now, between the ages of 3 and 4, he understands the idea, but *still* struggles and stumbles as he tries to comply. In fact, the major task of this year is learning to share and take turns. This is when that process really starts to gel. It's a task your child is working on in the company of his preschool teachers and peers, and one that goes easier with some enlightened parental intervention.

When your child says "No," you might say:

> **"I know that is your box of popcorn and I also know popcorn is one of your favorite treats. Maybe you can let Tim have a little and then maybe he can let you have some of his Reese's Pieces."**

And then let the matter drop. Don't insist. Give him time to respond. If you can, stay out of any subsequent hassling between the two children over the popcorn and the candy.

The idea: First, label what belongs to him ("that is your popcorn"); when he has a sense of ownership, he'll find it easier to move on to letting someone else use what is his. Second, gently suggest he let his pal have some. Then allow him to take it from there: He may share or he may not (and it really is all right to say "no" sometimes). If he does let his friend dig into the popcorn, later on—also gently, without making a huge deal of the matter—tell him it was nice that he shared, and Tim looked happy to have some popcorn to eat.

. . .

Two 3½-year-olds on a play date got into a shoving and hitting match over the one toy dump truck that each wanted to use. The host boy's father entered the scene and said:

> "Okay, there's one dump truck, you each want it, so here's what we'll do. I'm going to bring the cooking timer in here and set it to ring in five minutes. One of you can play with the truck now, and in five minutes when the timer goes off the other guy gets the truck."

The boys said they didn't want any timer. Dad replied:

> "If you don't want to use the timer, that's all right with me. We'll just put the truck away."

The children decided they'd use the timer after all. Dad directed the temporarily truckless child to another toy vehicle, and play went on fairly smoothly.

THE TOOLS: Be empathetic—it is <u>very</u> hard for a child this age to hand over his possessions. Don't push "sharing" down your child's throat. He knows what it's all about by this time, but it still doesn't come easily and he still needs lots of practice. If he manages it, notice his kind behavior and let him know it's appreciated—you're pleased with him, and the other kid looked happy too.

When you need to help kids work out taking turns, be a play date supervisor. Get the discontented child involved with a substitution. Remember that using a timer (a sort of neutral bad guy) can work wonders. Offer choices: Use a timer or don't play with the toy.

· · ·

One mother wanted to pass on some of her 4-year-old son's toys to his 2-year-old brother. Realizing that sharing his toys would be difficult for Anthony—and also that *she* would not be pleased to have someone else go through her things and decide which she wasn't using anymore—she said to her son:

> **"Anthony, I'd like you to look through your toys and choose those Thomas can use. I think you'll find some you don't play with anymore. If you're not sure which ones you want to share with him, you can think about it and take a few days to decide."**

Anthony said nothing at first, but a couple of days later he was willing to relinquish a few items. His mother approved his actions, his little brother was happy, and Anthony felt pretty good about the whole matter.

THE TOOLS: Set up success stories when you can. Present your child with a sharing task that he'll feel in control of and that you know he'll be able to manage.

GETS INTO SIBLING FIGHTS.

THE SCENE: Your 1½-year-old exuberantly smacks his 3½-year-old sister, who turns around and bops him right back. In a flash, the two are pushing, hitting, and crying.
THE BACKGROUND: Hitting is just one of many ways siblings show they're not thrilled with each other, which—if you're the parent of two children under age 5—you know all

too well. As a firstborn adjusts to the wrenching reality that now (and forevermore!) she must share her parents and most other aspects of her life with a younger brother or sister, she may be aggressive, or clingy and demanding, or babyish.

If your children are getting aggressively physical, resist the natural temptation to say to your oldest, "You're the big boy now, you know better than to hit." That sends the message that it might be smart to regress and act like "the little boy," because babies get away with things and have more privileges. Instead, say:

> **"Remember that hitting isn't allowed. Right now your brother doesn't have a lot of control and gets excited, but you still can't hit back. When he's older he won't hit so much."**

Don't let the 1½-year-old off the hook. Say:

> **"You can't hit either. If you want something, you can ask for it or point to it, okay?"**

As often as you can, try to be nearby and on the alert when the two are playing together so you can intervene if necessary and remind everybody of the "no rough stuff" rule. (After ages 4 or 5, they will have learned the skills that should enable them to settle disputes on their own.) It's a good idea, too, to keep your younger child out of your older child's play dates; tell your older child: "I'll make sure your brother is busy so you can have time with your friend."

THE TOOLS: In dealing with any sibling problems, be especially empathetic and understanding toward your older child, and you'll work wonders. Be a play date supervisor to keep hitting in control, and show the little tot how to use words and gentler actions to get what he wants.

. . .

The mother of 3½-year-old Keith says her son was sweet and affectionate to his newborn sister, but when the baby reached about 8 or 9 months of age and was becoming a real and very cute little "person," Keith suddenly wanted all his parents' attention. The clinginess drove both Mom and Dad crazy, especially at the end of the day: "I'm exhausted," says Mom, "and Keith is glued to my leg! I want to shout, 'Stop holding on to me all the time, you can't have me all to yourself!'"

But Mom didn't shout. During Keith's most clingy and needy phase, which went on for several months, she made a point of regularly telling Keith she understood what her son was going through. She said:

> "You know, it's really tough sometimes to have Gwen here when we used to have so much time just to ourselves."
>
> "Sometimes we just need extra hugs and kisses, don't we? Everybody needs extra hugs and kisses sometimes, so you just go ahead and ask me for them."
>
> "I know it's hard to say good night, but we're going to put the new book right here and it's going to be waiting for us tomorrow."

When Mom walked Keith to nursery school, they took a few minutes on the way to stop in a shop for coffee and juice. She was religious about giving her son "special time" each day, when the two of them played whatever Keith wanted, no interruptions. And sometimes after that, she cajoled Keith along into giving her "permission" to go to his sister:

"You know, Gwen has been really quiet in her playpen. I think she feels kind of bad right now that nobody's paying attention to her. What do you think we should do? Maybe I should do some things with her for a little while, like I've been doing with you."

THE TOOLS: Sharing Mom is the hardest thing! Clingy behavior will fade away if you empathize and show your older child you're on his side. Remember your 20 minutes of one-on-one time each day, one of the most effective tools for defusing sibling rivalry; when you tell your child, "I'm going to spend this time just with you," you can absolutely transform the relationship between you.

•   •   •

One mother said her 4-year-old daughter started showing regressive behavior when her baby brother began taking over some of her old possessions, like her stroller, crib, and high chair. Although Louise had been happily sitting at her own special small table in the kitchen, for example, suddenly she wanted her high chair back. Her mother said:

"I know you want to sit in your high chair, and we have to let Elliot use it too. What do you think we should do?"

Together they came up with a plan. Mom would wake Louisa up earlier so she could eat her breakfast in the high chair while her brother was having his bottle; then her brother could come in later and sit in the high chair for his cereal. The plan worked perfectly for two days; on the third day, Louise told her mom, "It's okay to let me sleep. I don't have to sit in the high chair anymore."

THE TOOLS: Empathize . . . and then help your child feel more in control by involving her in the solution to a problem. It takes time.

WANTS TO PLAY DOCTOR.

THE SCENE: Your neighbor's little boy is over for an afternoon of play with your daughter. You find the two 4-year-olds in the bathroom with their overalls and underpants off, checking out each other's bodies.

THE BACKGROUND: Around ages 3 or 4, a child is likely to get really curious about what other kids look like without clothes. Sometimes, too, they're just bored, and "playing doctor" seems like an interesting thing to do.

Put an end to the doctor game in the bathroom—young children who are innocently exploring their bodies can hurt each other by poking fingers or toy stethoscopes in a vagina or anus or pulling on genitalia.

But you should recognize that they clearly have questions about the differences between boys and girls, and see if you can acknowledge that curiosity without making a big production of it all. Belly buttons are good—and fairly safe— to talk about! You might say:

> "I think you two are really interested in seeing what each other looks like. You put your clothes back on and go in the living room, and let's talk about our belly buttons. Isn't that a funny little thing, that belly button? That's where we were attached to our mothers once upon a time."

Or if you feel that last line takes things a bit further than you want to go, you can simply say:

> **"Everybody has a belly button. When you get home, you can ask your mom or dad some questions about it."**

Then tell the other child's parent about the doctor game and what you said to the kids. Parents have different ways of handling sexuality issues, and it is wise to avoid any "how babies are made" talk with someone else's child. You haven't gone any further than the belly button, and most other parents will have no problem with that.

Four-year-old Jacob's mother was lying in bed very early one Saturday morning reading a magazine, wearing only pajama bottoms. Jacob unexpectedly walked in, stopped, and stood staring at her breasts. Mom didn't want to send her child a signal that his curiosity was wrong, by scrambling to cover up or ordering him out of the room. She decided to downplay the situation. She said:

> **"Hi, honey. Do you want to come and give me a good-morning hug?"**

Jacob replied, "I want to grab your boobs."
His mother, keeping her cool, said:

> **"Well, you can look at my breasts, but you can't grab them because that will hurt. Why don't you go in the kitchen and get out the orange juice, and I'll get dressed and be right with you."**

Later, she spoke to her son about his apparent curiosity about the difference between men and women:

> "I can see you're interested in the differences
> between boys and girls. Breasts are something
> women have."

Jacob said, "I have a penis." His mother replied:

> "Yes, boys have penises. If you have other
> questions, please ask me. I have a book you can
> look at that shows the differences."

After that, she asked Jacob to knock on her door before entering. She also made sure she was clothed if there was a chance Jacob would come in her room. If he did come in without knocking first, she'd ask him to please wait a moment while she got dressed.

Children this age are intrigued by what naked bodies look like. See if you can find a good children's book you can look at with your child, one that shows pictures of children in a playful way—perhaps swimming at the beach without their suits on. The important point: Satisfy your youngster's interest in a casual, natural way.

THE TOOLS: Privacy is expected: Insist on a knock on the door before your child enters your room. If you've had an incident of your child and his little friend playing doctor, be a close play date supervisor for a while and insist on one child using the bathroom at a time. Perhaps you can entertain the other a bit until the two friends get back together, and tell the child the closed bathroom door means one person at a time.

When your child is in a curious phase, channel his interest by providing information and giving him a "yes": He can look at picture books, he can ask you questions.

MAKES EMBARRASSING OBSERVATIONS ABOUT GROWN-UPS SHE SEES.

THE SCENE: As you're walking down the street, you notice your child is staring at a very overweight person coming toward you. As he passes, your youngster points to him and says, "He's fat."

THE BACKGROUND: Three- and four-year-olds find people's differences highly intriguing. Your child might blurt out: "She's so white." "He's so black." "Why is that lady yellow?" "That man has a big nose." She doesn't intend to be insulting or hurtful, she's simply making an accurate observation about a color, size, or other physical characteristic that she finds different and curious.

Such remarks, of course, are acutely embarrassing to you, the parent of this seemingly insulting child, especially when they've been made in a voice loud enough for all to hear. Here's how to handle the situation. Say to your child, without anger or immediate criticism:

> **"Susan, we'll talk about it later."**

Then, if possible, apologize to the offended adult—"I'm very sorry"—and move on.

Later, talk to your child:

> **"Susie, I know you didn't mean to hurt that man's feelings by saying he was very fat. Yes, he was fat, but I think it does hurt his feelings if people point to him and say he's fat."**

THE TOOLS: Model polite behavior for your child: When you offer a simple apology to someone who may have been offended by your child, you demonstrate one way of being sensitive to other people's feelings. And let her know the impact of her behavior—something she's said has had a probably unpleasant effect on someone else.

INTERRUPTS YOUR TALK WITH ANOTHER ADULT.

THE SCENE: You've just picked up your 3½-year-old from preschool, and as you're heading down the street you run into a couple of parent friends from the school. You stop to talk, but your child keeps interrupting, saying, "Mom! Mom!" and pulling on your arm and skirt.

THE BACKGROUND: Your child is excited to see you after a day at school and doesn't want to share you with anyone else. Also, she feels left out of the conversation.

Parents in my groups often report such encounters. When they ask their children to wait a minute while they're talking, the youngsters merely become more insistent, making the parents embarrassed in front of their friend and angry toward their children.

When you want your child to let you stop and chat with a friend, include her in the picture . . . first, with an introduction. Say to the friend:

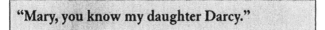

"Mary, you know my daughter Darcy."

There may follow a couple of "hellos" and smiles, and your child doesn't feel as if she's being pushed aside. Then tell her what's going to happen next:

> "Honey, Mrs. Smith and I are going to talk for a
> few minutes. Then you and I will go to the
> playground and we'll get something cool to drink."

Tell her she can skip ahead a little ways, as long as you can
still see her, or run in circles around you. Or pull out a book
for her to look at. If she still has trouble not interrupting, be
on your child's side. Pull her close to you, tell your friend
you're on the way to the playground and you'll call her later
to finish the conversation. Later, you might tell your daughter
that she needs to give you a few minutes to talk to a friend
sometimes, the same way you stop and let her spend a little
time with one of her friends when they meet on the street.

THE TOOLS: Tell your child what to expect; if she knows
she's going to get your undivided attention soon and you'll be
doing something fun together, she's likely to be more able to
wait. Let her know the impact of her behavior—she can make
it possible for you to enjoy some time with your friend, just as
you do for her. Model polite behavior: Make sure you introduce your child.

WHEN YOUR
4- TO
5-YEAR-OLD . . .

RESISTS YOUR REQUEST TO HELP OUT.

THE SCENE: You call to your 5-year-old to please come in the laundry room and help you deliver the clean clothes around to everybody's room. He doesn't answer and doesn't appear. After dinner you ask him to please stack the dishes on the sink counter. He doesn't do that either.

THE BACKGROUND: As we mentioned, a youngster may abruptly tire of familiar routines, including chores he once carried out willingly. But if your 4- or 5-year-old resists or gets resentful when you ask for help, something else may be going on.

A child this age seems suddenly so much more grown-up than previously, and his parents start expecting more "adult" behavior, like real participation in the work of the household.

That tendency is especially likely if a younger sibling is in the picture, so Mom and Dad are always busy and rushed, and the 5-year-old is "the big boy" who's supposed to be cooperative at all times. Those expectations may be too high.

．　　．　　．

If your child is ignoring your requests for help, think carefully about what it is you're asking of him and if it's too much. And then talk it over with him.

One mother came to the end of a long, frustrating Saturday when her husband was away on a business trip and she was managing their 3-year-old and less-than-agreeable 5-year-old. After the older child had balked at doing three or four cleanup chores, Mom said to him:

> "I need you to be more help to me right now. I know it's difficult sometimes to be the older brother and a lot is expected of you. Sometimes you want to be the little guy yourself. But if we help each other, everything will go a little better."

The son replied:

> "I don't want to do any of these things! Daddy doesn't have to do them. I'll only do what Daddy does."

Mom:

> "Well, Mommy's different. But it's more difficult when Daddy isn't here, so we have to help each other. Now, it sounds to me like I'm asking you to do too much, so let's figure out what has to get done and then we'll see how to handle it."

And then she ran down a short list of some things that would need to be accomplished the next day, and asked him to pick what he would do. Sunday went much more pleasantly, with her son following through on his decision to unpack groceries, feed the cats in the morning and the evening, and carry out two or three more chores. And Mom told him she really appreciated that. She told him how much difference his helping had made. The work was done in half the time, the cats were happier because they'd been fed, and there had been more time to play outdoors.

THE TOOLS: Be empathetic. Let your child know what's coming up and give him some choices as to how he'll participate— he's involved in solutions. And then praise him for a job well done.

LIKES SUPERHEROES AND ALL-POWERFUL TALK.

THE SCENE: Your child is enamored of Luke Skywalker. More than enamored: He seems to think he *is* Luke Skywalker, and he runs around slashing the air with his lightsaber and wears his Skywalker shirt morning, noon, and night.
THE BACKGROUND: Many children around ages 4 and 5 become caught up with a particular superhero, or with *all* superheroes, those powerful figures who never get scared and who beat up the bad guys. A child this age, with his burgeoning skills and knowledge of the world, feels pretty brash; he starts to think, "I can do so much, why can't I take charge of everything?" Love of superheroes comes from identifying with their aggressiveness and ability to take charge.
It also comes from the flip side of the child's brashness: "Uh-oh, I know I'm not really big enough to take charge . . . so my superhero can do it for me."

Superhero identification and tough-guy talk can be endearing and not troublesome to parents. They'll start to worry if the pretend behaviors seem to be taking over much of the youngster's time and thoughts.

Or they'll become annoyed—and nag the child to cut it out!—if those behaviors are driving them up the wall. One little boy saw *Terminator 2* starring supertough-guy Arnold Schwarzenegger (not a great choice of movie for a 4-year-old), and proceeded to say *"Hasta la vista,* baby!" to his parents about fifty times a day. They couldn't get him to stop. Finally, whenever he came out with another *"Hasta la vista,"* Mom and Dad put their fingers in their ears and left the room. The youngster got over it in time.

If your youngster does seem to be eating, drinking, and breathing Skywalker or Superman, if he insists on wearing the special shirt and carrying the special weapon all day long, if he demands you call him by his superhero name instead of his real name, if he wants to play only superhero games, and if all this is driving you crazy *and* making you worry about repetitive behavior, you can work with him to set some limits.

Say:

> **"I know you love your Superman shirt. Let's decide when is a good time to wear it. You can wear it here in the house and when we go to Grandma's. And you can wear it to bed at night if you want. When you go to school and on a play date, you'll wear your regular shirt."**

If he protests, there may be room for some further negotiations:

> **"Well, school is not a good place for your Superman clothes, but maybe once or twice a week you can have it on under your regular shirt. We'll try that and see how you like it."**

Help him get ready for a play date that *doesn't* involve Superman: Before his friend arrives, make some suggestions of other games they can play, and then get them started and monitor the activities. And then, make sure he gets lots of outdoor time.

Superheroes *can* be a force for good in your child's development. Spend some time reading stories together about other powerful, take-charge people whose heroics don't depend on leaping tall buildings in a single bound. He can see there are many ways to be strong.

THE TOOLS: Superhero behavior and all-powerful talk will die down. If it's getting on your nerves, use a little humor to keep your perspective and to get a (mild) point across to your child. Be a play date supervisor to encourage him to include other games in his day. Let him know he can "be" Superman sometimes (that's giving him a "yes") but not all the time, and give him choices about when that will be. Give him lots of outdoor time.

WANTS TO WIN AT GAMES ALL THE TIME.

THE SCENE: You and your youngster are having a good time playing Chutes and Ladders, but when you win she angrily flings the board and pieces over the floor. Or your child always wants to play Hungry, Hungry Hippos when her friend comes over because she's good at it and her friend isn't, so she's always the winner.
THE BACKGROUND: Children this age love winning; losing is frustrating *and* makes them upset and angry. Many parents I meet worry that "letting a child win" is a bad idea

because that's not real life, and that their child won't learn how to be a good sport. Don't worry—there's no harm done if Mom or Dad throws an occasional game (not all the time!). Your child will learn over time to temper her frustrations; you can help her along if you acknowledge her feelings about losing.

Suppose, in that Chutes and Ladders scenario, your child has just announced that she hates this game and doesn't want to play anymore. Say:

> **"I think you are hating this because I won two games. I know it's hard not to win and it seems unfair that I'm doing all the winning right now, but that's just the way these two games came out."**

Perhaps during another session your child wins a game, but she's still not happy because you won two. You can say:

> **"I'm really glad you won this game. I know it's hard not to win all the time. When you're trying to learn how to do something, it's difficult."**

By talking it through with her in this small way, you'll give her some perspective on what goes into playing a game and help her focus on the process rather than only on the end result. Besides, you're modeling desirable behavior: As pleasant as it is to come out on top yourself, you're happy when the other person is the winner sometimes.

See if in the future you might need to make your game-playing time shorter, so it doesn't become so frustrating. Sometimes, pick another game, like Memory, that your child is almost certain to do better at than you—little kids can always top us in memory games!

THE TOOLS: Let your child know you empathize with her feelings: You like to win too. Set up a little success story for her; play another game, one you know she's especially good at.

If your child is regularly getting into difficulties with a playmate over winning and losing, say:

> "Sure, you want to win that hippo game all the time, so you can understand how Robby feels when he comes over here and he's losing all the time. He doesn't like it, either. So for now, if you have to win all the time and he can't lose all the time, it looks like you'll have to play something else."

Child:

> "No, that's what I want to play."

You:

> "I know you do, but for now, pick out another activity you both can do. The hippo game is too hard for you, because Robby starts getting mad and upset, and we can't have him miserable. Maybe next week you can try that one again."

You might have to keep close watch over the next play date or two. If her little friend is again losing all the time and getting unhappy, remind your child about the agreement you made to stop and move on to another game.

THE TOOLS: Be empathetic: Although you disapprove of her behavior, you still understand her desire to win. Point out that her behavior has an impact on others. If she sets up playtime so that she always wins, her friend ends up unhappy and nobody really has much fun. Get her involved in the solution; ask her if she can figure out ahead of time what else they might do together. And make sure the new plan stays on track. Impose consequences: If one game makes someone unhappy, they must switch to another game.

IS DISRESPECTFUL TO PROPERTY.

THE SCENE: You've been caught up for hours in a major household spring cleaning. You walk into your bedroom and discover that your 4-year-old is using her colored markers to decorate your white bedspread.

THE BACKGROUND: Young children, in the course of growing up, are sometimes going to scribble on walls, break lamps, or in other ways damage property. Usually, they do so accidentally, or mindlessly, or because they haven't yet learned how and where to use art supplies, balls, and other playthings. Occasionally, something else—anger at being pushed aside or frustration over being constantly warned not to "make a mess"—may be behind the destructive behavior.

The sight of your garishly marked-up bedspread naturally sends you into a fit. You're likely to order your child into her room, with a stern reprimand.

While you're cooling off, give some thought to what happened. Was your child sitting on your bed doodling on her drawing pad, and then did she become exuberantly carried away with her efforts and decide her artwork would look nice on your bedspread? Or was she trying, fruitlessly, to get your attention all day?

Apply a little democratic discipline. Say:

> "Maddie, you know you have to use markers on your drawing paper. I got very upset when I saw my bed. This bedspread has to be cleaned up now. Suppose you help me take it off the bed, and we'll put this in the washing machine with some soap and see if we can get it clean."

Do involve your child in repairing damage she's caused, not as a punishment but as a way of showing that her responsibilities to the family include trying to fix a problem she's created.

Very possibly, your youngster wanted to have a little more of your attention. While you're working on that cleanup job together, you might say:

> "I know I've been doing spring cleaning for a long time today. If you want me to do something with you, you just tell me. Sometimes I forget if I'm busy, but you can ask me for things. You can tell me if it's time for me to stop."

And think of some actions you can take that might prevent a repeat performance of the marked-up-bedspread kind of behavior: Can you tape some giant sheets of inexpensive construction paper to her wall, so she can make a big, scribbly mural? Have you put too much of your house "off-limits" to playtime, because you don't want things broken or dirtied? Have you explained to her where she *can* play and roughhouse and "make a mess"?

THE TOOLS: First, cool off and let your anger simmer down. Then, let her know the impact of her behavior—tell her you really were upset at the sight of that bedspread. Give her a consequence to her action and get her involved in a solution to make the situation better—for example, helping with the laundry! Give her words to use—"You can tell me to stop." And give her a "yes" by showing where she can make doodles to her heart's content.

ACTS UNRULY IN A PUBLIC PLACE.

THE SCENE: You, your spouse, and your 4-year-old have joined friends at a restaurant. You're looking forward to a pleasant evening out, which your child proceeds to demolish by knocking over the water glasses, slithering up and down the booth, whining, and interrupting conversations.
THE BACKGROUND: Young children can manage only a short time being polite and quiet when they're part of "grown-up" activities of little interest to them. This, of course, is just when you're perhaps most eager for your child to be on good behavior . . . and most likely to try to nag him into it.

When things are going from bad to worse at the restaurant, you or your spouse will have to give your child (and your dinner companions) a break by taking him out for a walk or a trip to the bathroom, and then, perhaps, draw the evening to an earlier close than you had planned. To avoid or curtail unpleasant public scenes in the future, your best offense is a good defense. Plan some preventive actions and let your child know what they are.

One mother was meeting a friend for a restaurant lunch and movie afterward, and wanted to bring her 4-year-old. A similar previous outing had been a disaster, with lots of complaining from the little girl. This time her mom said:

> "Last time we went out I didn't like hearing all that whining, and you know that it was very hard for me to hold my temper. Today I've planned something nice for the two of us with Mrs. Adams. We can take your toy pony and your coloring book, and you can use them at the restaurant. Then we'll see how you feel during lunch and if you're ready to go on to the movie. If you find it's just too hard for you, I'll bring you back home and you can stay next door with Pammy while I go to the movie. It will be your choice."

She then did try to include her daughter in the conversation at lunch. All went well for the entire afternoon.

Tell your child what to expect and involve him in the game plan. Say:

> "When we get to dinner, you'll be sitting for a while and the other people will expect you to sit there and be pretty quiet. We're going to bring your book, but I think even with the book it will be hard for you to sit still after a while. So you give me a signal. You can tap the salt shaker or wiggle your fingers. And then Dad or I will take you out for a walk."

One father took his son to church services each Sunday, and helped him sit through the service without squirming by allowing him to bring a book or coloring pad and markers. But he also wanted him to pay attention to certain parts of the service. He told him:

> "When we get to church you can read and draw with your markers. You don't have to listen all the time. When we get to the part I want you to hear, I'll let you know and you can give me your book to hold, and then afterward I'll let you get back to it."

Later, he told his son he was really happy that the child was able to amuse himself for a while and then listen for a while.

THE TOOLS: Your child must be respectful to the people around him in a restaurant, church, synagogue, or other public place. Help him along by telling him what to expect, by empathizing ("It's going to be hard for you to sit still"), and by being on his side and offering choices ("You can sit here and read your book, or listen to us talk, or we'll take a walk outside for a few minutes"). When he handles it, praise him for a job well done.

EXPRESSES CRITICISM OF ADULTS WITH RUDENESS OR THREATS.

THE SCENE: Your neighbor, a lovely woman whom your 5-year-old likes, comes over for an afternoon cup of tea and a chat. Your child doesn't answer her greeting. Worse, he tells her, "I don't want you to come in."

THE BACKGROUND: Life can get tough for the 4- to 5-year old. On the one hand, he enjoys new autonomy and powers; he's really got it together now when it comes to dressing himself, opening the refrigerator and getting out his own snack, throwing balls and catching them. He's feeling cocky and in charge.

On the other hand, this is when his parents—seeing this suddenly more grown-up child—start getting on his case about more grown-up behavior. They urge him to be less noisy in public, to be neater and cleaner, to say hello and shake hands and smile. He resists; one way he can feel he's still in charge is to respond to their demands by being rude or threatening.

When your child tells your friend to go away or refuses to say hello, it's embarrassing. You may be tempted to reprimand him on the spot: "That's not a nice thing to say" or "When somebody you know says hello, you should say hello back." You may be tempted to excuse his behavior: "Johnny's had a cold, he's feeling kind of cranky today."

Don't pressure yourself or your child. If you and your spouse are polite and respectful to others, Johnny will be too, in time. Faced with the embarrassing moment, ignore the rudeness and redirect your child's attention:

> "Johnny, Mrs. Garcia and I are going to visit for a while. Let's get your Brio trains out so you can build a set. Or would you rather play with your Legos? Come on, I'll help you get things set up. Later, we'll go out to the pet store like we planned and pick up that new birdseed we talked about."

If you can get your child set up like this *before* your visitor arrives, you'll be in even better shape.

Later, on your way to the pet store, you might calmly tell your child that you think Mrs. Garcia felt bad when he told her not to come in, but you and she had a nice visit and you were pleased that he could occupy himself for a while.

One mother was repeatedly annoyed by her $4^{1}/_2$-year-old's threats, which took the form of "If you don't let me . . . then I won't. . . ." These confrontations usually ended with Mom barking orders and son sullenly obeying. One evening, the mother tried a different route. Her son said:

> **"I want to stay up to finish my drawing. If I can stay up later, I'll get all dressed by myself tomorrow. If I can't stay up, I'm never going to dress myself."**

Mom, ignoring the threat, replied:

> **"Okay, let's give it a try."**

Came the morning and time to leave for school, the little boy wasn't dressed. *Now* he wanted candy and told Mom if he didn't get candy he'd never get himself dressed. Mom kept her cool and said:

> **"Candy and clothes have nothing to do with each other. And this is the time for clothes, not candy. You know, last night you told me if I let you stay up later you'd get yourself ready this morning. I know you'll put your clothes on eventually, because everybody has to get dressed eventually. Right now I'm going to get you dressed because we're late, and we can't have candy now or staying up tonight."**

Mom felt good, because she didn't give in to an unreasonable demand and because this episode hadn't turned into one of their nagging/bossing matches. She also found other small ways to give her child more power during his day, so he didn't need to gain power by threats and not doing what she needed him to do.

THE TOOLS: Ease up on your 4- to 5-year-old; he wants to feel in control, so let him make as many choices throughout his day as are compatible with a fairly smooth-flowing family life. Don't try to correct rudeness with instant reprimands, but do let him know that it makes other people feel bad when he behaves that way. When he <u>does</u> occupy himself and cooperates, commend him afterward.

SAYS "I HATE YOU!" OR "YOU'RE SO STUPID!"

THE SCENE: Your 5-year-old has been in no mood to cooperate since the moment she opened her eyes this morning. Nothing you do is right; matters have been going from unpleasant to impossible. When you tell her, politely, that you've already asked her twice to empty out her backpack and bring her lunch box into the kitchen, she shouts, "I hate you! You're stupid!"

THE BACKGROUND: This is a real button-pusher for parents. It feels bad to hear such words from your child! It hurts *and* it makes you see red. Remind yourself that she does not *really* hate you or think you're stupid. Perhaps other kids were giving her grief all day, she's angry and tired, she wants more control of her life right now. But when it comes to handling all those feelings, she still has only a limited repertoire.

Remind yourself of this too: We encourage our children to use words instead of hands, teeth, or feet to express unhappy feelings. Then they use words we don't like. They use them because, partly, they see by our reactions there's power in those words. And partly, they may not be entirely sure what the words mean.

When you're the butt of such an outburst from your child, resist the perfectly normal impulse to shout back, "Don't you talk to me that way, go to your room right now and stay there until I tell you to come out." Instead, take five. Give yourself time to cool off. Then you might say:

> **"You were pretty mad at me back there. It's okay to be angry. Everybody gets angry. But it really hurts my feelings when you say those things to me. If you want to tell me that you don't like something that I'm doing, I'll listen."**

If she has no response to that suggestion (and she probably won't), you might take things a step further and ask her if something else happened during the day to make her feel angry. Don't belabor the point if she has nothing she wants to say; you're giving her a little gentle encouragement to describe her feelings rather than express them through insults and attack words.

Or, talk about the words:

> **"I think you need to know what that word 'hate' means. You might hate someone who's being really mean to a little kitten. He hits the kitten or he won't feed it or he leaves it out in the cold. You might hate that person because he's doing things that are mean and cruel."**

One mother had had it hearing from her little son how stupid she was. She said to him:

> **"Listen, I'm going to tell you right now what stupid means. Stupid means that you see a bus coming down the street and you run in front of**

> it. Stupid means you're cutting up an apple and you put your finger right where the knife is going to go. That's stupid! Stupid doesn't mean somebody made a mistake or forgot to do something."

Her son said, "Okay, *okay*, Mom." He still said, "You're stupid," occasionally, but each time he'd giggle; finally, there were no more stupids.

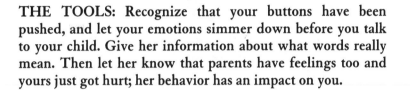

THE TOOLS: Recognize that your buttons have been pushed, and let your emotions simmer down before you talk to your child. Give her information about what words really mean. Then let her know that parents have feelings too and yours just got hurt; her behavior has an impact on you.

LIKES TOILET TALK AND SWEARING.

THE SCENE: "Peepee, poopoo, peepee, poopoo, you're a peepee poopoo face!" shouts your 4-year-old.

THE BACKGROUND: Four- and five-year-olds love saying words that they know will get a rise out of the grown-ups. Kids learn that language has power, because we keep telling them to use words; then they figure out that some words aggravate or surprise their parents, and that gives them a feeling of control—what an interesting response they get from Mom and Dad!

Toilet talk also can be part of the language of children, a funny way for them to talk to each other. Swearing often has to do with hearing words and not knowing what they mean, except that they're powerful because people use them when they're angry or upset.

If your child finds it irresistible to call you or her older brother or sister a peepee face, don't nag her to stop. For whatever reason, this is something she needs to do right now. (Maybe she's feeling a little left out of things or overshadowed by that older sibling.) Put limits on the behavior and then try to ignore it as much as possible. Say:

> "You know, Mom and I would like to have you here in the living room with us, but not when you're talking like that. If you want to say those things, you'll have to do it in your room, and then when you're finished, come on out and we'll think of something to do together."

She may stand right in her bedroom door and carry on with the peepee-poopoo-face talk for 10 minutes. Pay no attention, and most likely she'll emerge in a while and be just fine.

After listening to some construction work going on in the street outside his house, a 4-year-old went to the window and—in his lispy, little-boy voice—shouted, "Shut up, you fuckin' bathtards, you're making too much noithe!"

His mom said firmly:

> "Those words are not nice to use, so let's not have any more of them."

She realized that he'd probably picked up the words from his father, who often got short-tempered and hotheaded while they were out driving and stuck in traffic! So she also talked to her husband and he made an effort to clean up his language.

If you're sure you or your spouse isn't the example, find out if your child is being set up by older kids. If your youngster is in kindergarten and riding a school bus every day, possibly the 12- and 13-year-olds are egging him on. Say:

> **"Those are a lot of strong words. Where did you hear them?"**

If, indeed, he tells you the bigger boys on the school bus say them, you can say:

> **"Well, that's really not the way we talk. Those kids may think it's funny, but we don't think it's so funny around here. So no more."**

You may choose to explain to your child the meaning of the words he's using, which is fine if you keep it simple and unemotional:

> **"That's a street word or a rough word for something nice grown-ups do when they care for each other. It's not a good word to use when you're angry or annoyed about something."**

THE TOOLS: Ignore the offensive talk as much as possible, but if it goes on, give your child limits and consequences: If she must talk that way, she has to do it in her own room (that's giving a "yes") or in the bathroom, and she doesn't get to spend time with you. Plan joint approaches with your spouse: Both parents need to be aware of the language they use.

ACTS BOSSY OR IGNORES YOU.

THE SCENE: You're talking to your 5-year-old and she behaves as if you're not even there. Other times, she orders you around like a drill sergeant.
THE BACKGROUND: Four- and five-year-olds are obstinate people. They often react to Mom and Dad or other people in ways that say, "I do not see or hear you right now," or "I'm calling the shots here." Sometimes they ignore you entirely; sometimes they're impossibly bossy.

When your child doesn't hear you, do some role-playing. Here's how that might go:

> Mom: **"You're ignoring me, and that makes me feel bad. Do you know how you'd feel if I ignored you? Let's try it. You say something to me."**
> Child: **"Hi, Mom."**
> Mom: **"Hmm . . . hmmm . . . hmm."**
> Child: **"Mom . . . Mom!"**

Ask your child how she felt; she just might acknowledge it didn't feel very good to be ignored.

One father always read a book to his 4½-year-old at night, a bedtime routine they both enjoyed. While he started reading one evening, his son looked through a comic book. Dad asked him, twice, to please put the comic book down; his requests fell on deaf ears. Finally, he said:

> **"I feel like the invisible man here. I've asked you twice to put your comic down, and I'm being ignored. I know you'd like me to read you a story, but you're not helping and my feelings are getting hurt."**

His son apologized. "Sometimes I don't think," he said.

THE TOOLS: Let your child know the impact of his behavior on you . . . when he ignores you, you feel hurt.

.   .   .

Several 4½-year-olds were playing a game of house during a party, and one youngster was running the show. She announced who would be the mother, the father, the grandmother, the pet dog; when one child decided she was tired of being the grandmother, the leader of the pack said, "It's *my* game, I pick what you have to be."

When children reach ages 4 and 5, parents can usually step back and let them solve their own problems. But if during play one youngster is being bossy and making another upset, a parent can give the unhappy child words to use. At this party, Mom took his daughter aside and said:

> **"If you don't want to play that or you don't want to be the grandmother anymore, say to Gretchen, 'I don't like this . . . that's not what I'm going to be.' "**
> Child: **"But she'll tell me she won't play."**
> Mom: **"If that happens, you can say, 'All right, I don't want to play house either, I'm going to play something else.' "**

THE TOOLS: When one child's bossiness is interfering with play, it's best not to jump in and bail the youngsters out of their difficulties. But you can give a child words to use to try to make the situation better for herself. If things don't improve, the bossy child may learn that the consequence of her behavior is that nobody wants to play and the game ends.

Chapter 5

KEEPING UP THE PROGRESS:

Good ways to maintain positive parenting.

BEING A PARENT, RAISING THE next generation, is the most important job any of us has. This book has been designed to help you do the best job possible. As you guide your child along his road to independence through his first five years, using the tools of democratic discipline, here are some ideas on keeping up the progress:

From time to time, reread the tools. When you're learning to play golf, even after you've become pretty good at it, your game improves even further if you take a lesson every now and then. In the same way, rereading the tools will refresh your memory on the basics of positive parenting, and remind you of the attitudes and actions you want to keep in play.

Also, children grow and change. If you're now the parent of a 1-year-old, you may find it not only helpful but surprising to go back and reread the tools when your child is 2½ or 3. You'll come at them with a little different understanding or perspective. Some tools that seemed mainly of academic interest when your son or daughter was younger will pop out with new meaning and relevance.

And you need to give yourself hope too, repeatedly! Several of the tools are not about what to do with your child, but about how to be kind to yourself and how to keep an eye on long-term goals and the big picture. That's a message you need to keep hearing.

Join a parenting group. Many churches, synagogues, schools, local Y's, child-care centers, and other institutions routinely schedule workshops, groups, or talks on parenting issues. Take advantage of them.

As you meet with other parents, you compare notes, gain insights, reinforce what you are doing well. You learn what to expect from children as a whole, see how others have handled problems, get questions answered, and make some friends. That kind of support and perspective is invaluable, because parents can't be loners.

Keep in contact with another parent (or several) whose views are similar to yours and whose child is about the same age as yours. Call this parent during rough times; you'll get understanding, you'll let off a little steam, and you'll hang up the phone feeling better and with a refreshed attitude toward your child.

That's another kind of support that is priceless. I know from personal experience that often you need to get by with a little help from your friends!

Expect to have discouraging days as a parent. Sometimes your best efforts are for naught. Sometimes your child will not be satisfied or happy with his lot in life. And that will not necessarily have a whole lot—or anything at all—to do with you and the quality of your parenting. It may have everything to do with your child's age or stage or the day he's having or with his innate temperament.

Read other child-raising books. I've provided in the next section a list of books that I've found helpful and that I often recommend to the mothers and fathers who come to my workshops. Few of us are trained to be parents. Child-raising books can help you get some training, especially in the all-important matter of keeping expectations in line with a child's capabilities.

What I've been calling democratic discipline is a challenge! It takes time and effort (although less time and effort, as you and your child get better at it). But the rewards are immense. And they are felt in two ways.

First, as said, the day-to-day struggles decrease. There's less nagging and more fun.

And, second, here's the real payoff. By following the principles of *Tired of Nagging?*, you've encouraged your young child to participate in the solutions to his own problems. You've helped him figure out ways to manage himself. And because of that, when he moves into the preteen and teen years he has an excellent foundation for making his own judgment calls in the face of peer pressures and for finding the direction he needs to go in. You've also raised a child who is capable of being empathetic toward you and others.

In thinking about that wonderful payoff somewhere down the line, I was reminded of a couple of parents who have participated in my workshops, and of stories they've told me recently.

Ten-year-old Meredith shared with her teacher one day a number of gripes she had about her 13-year-old brother, whom she was usually quite fond of. He acted superior, Meredith said, because he was really good at a lot of things. Sometimes she disliked sharing the same house with him.

And then she added: "I think I'm jealous of Brian! But you know, I don't really know why I am. He doesn't get any more attention than I do. My mom spends a lot of time with me. She walks me to school. We go shopping together and we often go out to lunch together on Saturdays. There's no reason for me to be jealous of Brian, but I am!"

The teacher, impressed by the girl's keen sense of what was going on in her own head and heart, repeated this conversation to Meredith's mother, who told it to me. "And a day later," said Meredith's mother with a laugh, "the two kids were happily working on a computer project together. The storm had passed!"

Jonathan's mother had planned a Saturday outing for the two of them, a visit to the model hobby shop and lunch. She also had scheduled a repairman to do some work in their apartment that morning, and as things turned out, the household work took up most of the day. In exasperation, she said to her son, "I'm so dumb! I shouldn't have started that project today. We can't have any fun now."

Ten-year-old Jonathan said, "You're not dumb, Mom. You just got mixed up!"

Mom: "But we don't have time to do what we planned!"

Jonathan said: "Come on, Mom. We'll do something else tonight to have fun."

She gave her son a hug, she told me, and she felt so happy that Jonathan had been able to give her this loving "reprieve."

One child could put her finger on her own feelings, see where they were coming from, and give a passing salute of appreciation to her parent. One child was able to see beyond his own disappointment and cheer up his mom.

Those parents, I thought, had got it down right! Their children could act considerately because they were helped by parents who showed empathy, redirected energy to positive action, got them involved in solutions, and showed appreciation for all the fine strides they made along the way.

That's what happens when you treat your child with the innate respect that's at the core of democratic discipline—you get it back.

NOTES

CHAPTER 2: BEHAVIORAL AGES AND STAGES

1, page 8
- Lief, Nina R., M.D., *The First Year of Life* (New York: Walker Publishing Co., Inc., 1991), pp. 146 and 249. This book was one of my main sources for the developmental characteristics of children aged 6 months to 1 year.

2, page 8
- Ibid, p. 252
- Caplan, Theresa and Frank, *The Early Childhood Years: The 2- to 6-Year-Old* (New York: Bantam Books, 1984). This book was one of the main sources for the developmental characteristics of children aged 2 through 4 years.
- Erikson, Erik, *Childhood and Society* (New York: W.W. Norton and Company, Inc., 1993), pp. 247–248.

3, page 9
- Caplan, Theresa and Frank, *The Second Twelve Months of Life* (New York: Bantam Books, 1985), p. 243. This book was one of the main sources of developmental characteristics for children aged 6 months to 2 years.

- Nina Lief, pp. 126–127
- White, Burton, *The First Three Years of Life* (New York: Prentice Hall Press, 1985), p. 133.

4, page 11
- Oppenheim, Joanne, Betty Boeghold, and Barbara Brenner, *Raising a Confident Child* (New York: Pantheon Books, 1989), pp. 66–67.

5, page 12
- Lief, Nina R., M.D., *The Second Year of Life* (New York: Walker Publishing Company, Inc., 1991), p. 136–137.

6, page 12
- Lief, Nina R., M.D., *The Third Year of Life* (New York: Walker Publishing Company, Inc., 1991), p. 142. This book was one of the sources for developmental characteristics of children aged 2 to 3 years.

7, page 14
- Oppenheim, Joanne, et al., pp. 104–105.

For developmental characteristics of children aged 2 through 4 years, these books by Louise Bates Ames and Francis L. Ilg were some of the sources:
- *Your Two-Year-Old: Terrible or Tender* (New York: Dell Publishing, 1970)
- *Your Three-Year-Old: Friend or Enemy* (New York: Dell Publishing, 1985)
- *Your Four-Year-Old: Wild and Wonderful* (New York: Dell Publishing, 1976)

CHAPTER 3: THE 30 PARENTING TOOLS

For the tool Praise Your Child, p. 31
- Ginott, Dr. Haim, *Between Parent and Child* (New York: Avon Books, 1965), pp. 44–52. Some ideas regarding the use of praise were drawn from this book.

For the tools Empathize, p. 35, and Wait Until The Emotions Have Settled, p. 36
- Briggs, Dorothy Corkville, *Your Child's Self-Esteem* (New York: Doubleday & Co., 1970), pp. 104–111. Some aspects about empathy were drawn from this book.

For the tool Consequences, p. 45
- Dreikurs, Dr. Rudolf, with Vicki Soltz, R.N., *Children: The Challenge* (New York: E.P. Dutton, 1964), pp. 76–85. Some ideas regarding the use of consequences were drawn from this work.

SUGGESTED READING

HERE IS A LIST OF books I like and recommend to my workshop parents for further reading.

One star (*): a book that can be shared with your child.

Two stars (**): if you have time for just one, this is the book I'd suggest.

GENERAL CHILD DEVELOPMENT

- Ames, Louise Bates, and Francis L. Ilg.
  Your Two-Year-Old. New York: Dell Publishing, 1980.
  *Your Three-Year-Old.*** New York: Dell Publishing, 1980.
  *Your Four-Year-Old.*** New York: Dell Publishing, 1989.
- Caplan, Theresa and Frank.
  The Early Childhood Years: The 2- to 6-Year-Old. New York: Bantam Books, 1984.
  The Second Twelve Months of Life. New York: Bantam Books, 1985 (8th printing).

- Leif, Nina R., M.D.
  *The First Year of Life.*** New York: Walker Publishing Co., Inc., 1991.
  *The Second Year of Life.*** New York: Walker Publishing Co., Inc., 1991.
  *The Third Year of Life.*** New York: Walker Publishing Co., Inc., 1991.

SELF-ESTEEM

- Branden, Nathaniel. *Honoring the Self: The Psychology of Confidence and Respect.* New York: Bantam Books, 1985.
- Briggs, Dorothy Corkville. *Your Child's Self-Esteem: The Key to His Life.*** New York: Doubleday Books, 1975. (This is my favorite book. Each time I reread it, I gain something new.)

DISCIPLINE

- Dreikurs, Rudolf, M.D. (with Vicki Soltz, R.N.). *Children: The Challenge.* New York: NAL Dutton, 1987.
- Mitchell, Grace. *A Very Practical Guide to Discipline with Young Children.*** Telshare Publishing, Inc., 1982. (Available at Bank Street College Bookstore, New York. Good for children up to age 5.)
- Nelson, Jane. *Positive Discipline.* New York: Ballantine Books, 1996 (revised edition). (Good for children aged 3 to 12.)

COMMUNICATION

- Faber, Adele, and Elaine Mazlish. *How to Talk So Kids Will Listen & Listen So Kids Will Talk.*** New York: Avon Books, 1982.
- Ginott, Haim. *Between Parent and Child.* New York: Avon Books, 1976.

TOILET TRAINING

- Borgardt, Marianne. *What Do You Do with a Potty?: An Important Pop-up Book.** Santa Monica, CA: Western Publishing Co., Inc., 1994.

- Cole, Joanna. *Parents' Book of Toilet Teaching.* New York: Ballantine Books, 1986.
- Schaefer, Charles E., and Theresa F. DiGeronimo. *Toilet Training Without Tears.* New York: Signet Books, 1989.

MORALITY DEVELOPMENT

- Damon, William. *The Moral Child: Nurturing Children's Natural Moral Growth.* New York: The Free Press, 1992.
- Markova, Dawna, et al., eds. *Random Acts of Kindness.** Berkeley, CA: Conari Press, 1993.
- Piper, Watty. *The Little Engine That Could.** New York: Putnam Publishing Group (Platt & Munk Publishers), 1984.
- Schulman, Michael, and Eva Mekler. *Bringing Up a Moral Child: A New Approach for Teaching Your Child to Be Kind, Just and Responsible.*** New York: Addison-Wesley Publishing Co., Inc., 1985.

SEXUALITY DEVELOPMENT

- Andry, Andrew, and Steven Schepp. *How Babies Are Made.* New York: Little, Brown & Co., 1984.
- Kuskin, Karla. *The Philharmonic Gets Dressed.** New York: HarperCollins Children's Books, 1982.
- Pearse, Patricia. *See How You Grow.** New York: Barron's Educational Series, Inc., 1988.
- Stein, Sara Bonnett. *Making Babies.** New York: Walker and Co., 1974. (My favorite book to share with your child; this title is out of print, but you may be able to find it in your library.)

SIBLINGS

- Ames, Louise Bates, and Carol C. Haber. *He Hit Me First: When Brothers and Sisters Fight.* New York: Warner Books, 1989.
- Faber, Adele, and Elaine Mazlish. *Siblings Without Rivalry: How to Help Your Children Live Together So You Can Live Too.* New York: Avon Books, 1988.

- Hoban, Russell.
  *A Birthday for Frances.** New York: HarperCollins
    Children's Books, 1968.
  *A Baby Sister for Frances.** New York: HarperCollins
    Children's Books, 1964.
- Lansky, Vicki. *Welcoming Your Second Baby*. Deephaven,
  Minnesota: The Book Peddlers, 1990 (revised edition).
- Reit, Seymour V. *Sibling Rivalry*. New York: Ballantine
  Books, 1988.
- Rogers, Fred. *The New Baby.** New York: Berkley Books,
  1996.

INDEX

ABOUT THE AUTHORS

VIRGINIA K. STOWE, M.S.N., is a parent adviser and family counselor with twenty-five years' experience in the field of parent-child education. She is the founder and director of Parenting Resource Center, Inc.; the founder of the first Sibling Group at the Early Childhood Development Center of New York Medical College; a contributing editor at *Working Mother* magazine; and a lecturer and workshop leader at many New York schools. She has conducted parenting seminars for employees at Sotheby's Inc. and other private companies.

Stowe has appeared on the TV show "Sexuality in Children," hosted by Jill Clayburgh, on cable TV's America's Talking, and on WINS 1010 and Success radio.

She earned her M.S.N. from the University of Pennsylvania and did postgraduate training in parent-family counseling under a National Institute Grant at Harvard Medical School. As part of this work, she taught parents interventions to assist their children's development, and methods for reducing family conflict and establishing a support system.

ANDREA THOMPSON was child-care and articles editor at *McCall's* magazine, and is a freelance writer specializing in parenting and women's issues. Her articles have appeared in many national magazines, including *Good Housekeeping, Redbook, Working Mother,* and *Parents.* She was ghostwriter for the book *Familyhood* by Dr. Lee Salk (Simon & Schuster, 1992) and is co-author of the books *Maternal Fitness,* with Julie Tupler, R.N. (Fireside, 1996), and *You and Your Only Child,* with Patricia Nachman, Ph.D. (Harper Perennial, 1998).

Printed in the United States
by Baker & Taylor Publisher Services